JUVENILE DELINQUENCY

A CALL FOR DIVINE INTERVENTION

Paul Campbell

Juvenile Delinquency
Published through Lulu Enterprises, Inc.

Cover Design by Carrie Lantry

Interior Book Design and Layout by
www.integrativeink.com

ISBN: 978-0-6152-3850-0

All scriptures have been taken out of the NKJV

DEDICATION

I dedicate this book to the Father, Son, and the Holy Spirit. It is the "FATHER" who has enabled me to pursue this level of theological study, and it is imperative that I give Him all the glory and honor for His knowledge, understanding, and wisdom, which He imparted into me. God has given me the vision, motivation, and endurance to run the race of Christianity as a minister of the gospel of Jesus Christ. God has encouraged me at times when I felt that it was impossible to complete this task and challenge. He has taught me that a true solider of His remains unmovable in spite of the many circumstances, situations, and relationships that one experiences within the Christian walk!

ACKNOWLEDGMENTS

I thank all of my ministerial colleagues for their spiritual support and Love. I thank my entire family unite. I would also like to thank my three daughters, Genesis, Naomi and Hannah who have brought extreme happiness and blessings to both my wife and I. Passionately, I thank my wife Keisha, who God has blessed me as my helpmate! I thank Keisha for her patience and acceptance for who I am and for standing with me through the peaceful, calm, and stormy moments that life offers one. I thank God who has given me permission to write this book. I thank Him for His holy preservation over my life and the life of my family, as well as for choosing me to be a minister of the gospel of Jesus Christ.

TABLE OF CONTENTS

PREFACE

There have been many events that have encouraged me to write this book. As a child, I was raised in a Christian home. However, the opportunity of becoming a juvenile delinquent and displaying destructive behavior was accessible. I can recall bringing a pocket-knife to a private elementary school—one that my parents purchased for me when I was to attend summer camp. Why I felt it so necessary to bring this knife to school, I really don't know! I asked the teacher for permission to use the restroom that morning, and when I went to the restroom, a student in my class was present and began agitating me. So, I took out the pocketknife that was in my blue school pants and cut my peer on the finger with the knife, and his finger began to bleed. I became shocked when I saw the blood gushing down his finger, and I knew that I was in big trouble with my teacher, principle, and most of all, my parents! The teacher found out and sent me straight to the principle's office where I was told I would be suspended from school. I would say that the school suspension was not the difficult part. However, the difficult part came when I went home and was corrected by my parents.

I would say that my parents were a little on the strict side, and now that I look back, I realize why. I had to be in bed at 8:30 P.M. during the weekdays and 9 P.M. during weekends. I think my siblings and I were the only family on the block that had to be in bed that early. I can recall violating my curfew one weekday when my mother instructed me to return to the house after she gave me additional hours to play with my peers in the neighborhood. Well, I decided to go over the time allotted and remained outside for an extra hour. When I returned home, I was placed on punishment for my disobedience.

As an adolescent, I never looked at the fact that my peers stayed out as long as they wanted to, regardless of how dark it was, or what possible opportunity for criminal activity existed. During my adolescent experiences, I found it challenging for many youths to remain on the pathways of righteousness. Many of the adolescents had no natural father in their home to guide and lead them in the direction that was of God. I find that it's more difficult and challenging for many of today's adolescents.

As we have entered the new millennium, one can see that there are many challenges that will arise. The world has become dominated by sin. In today's society, homes have become broken, parents are not conforming to their parental responsibilities, children are not complying with domestic rules and regulations, and adolescents are cleavings to criminal activity in multiple communities. It appears that the arrest rate of individuals eighteen years old or younger for violent crimes has increased dramatically.

Many researchers and professionals are searching for a solution among the juvenile delinquency population. Juvenile delinquents are searching for a remedy in their lives, someone or something to help them alleviate the internal pain that they are experiencing. There are some juveniles who believe that drugs can negate the pain; there are others professionals who believe that education is the right answer; and there are those juveniles who believe that money is the solution. It is evident that God does not want us to have pain, and ultimately, he will take it away from us!

> *And God will wipe away every tear from their eyes; there shall be no more death, no sorrow, nor crying. There shall be no more pain, for the former things have passed away. (Revelation 21:4)*

This book is designed to discuss a variety of things that contribute to juvenile delinquency. It is important to be aware that the objective of this book is to discuss matters pertaining to juvenile delinquency and the call for Divine Intervention. Juvenile delinquency is defined as any adolescent who engages in behavior that is contrary to the law. Divine Intervention is defined as a spiritual being that mediates a situation, circumstance, or relationship. To be more specific, the Divine Intervention is Jesus Christ.

CHAPTER 1
DISCUSSING TODAY'S GENERATION

In order to reach adolescents of today's generation, we must be able to enhance our ability to relate to their culture. In today's society, adolescents have begun to find their identity in fashion styles, rhetoric, and language. Hip-hop culture is displaying distinct styles of dress, language, and music and has been advancing since it came to development in the early 1990s. Although many individuals believe that this fashion trend is only prevalent in the urban communities, this is not necessarily the truth! Many of the hottest trends in teenage music, language, and fashion starts in America's inner cities, then quickly spreads to the suburbs.

There are some youths who become highly influenced by rap artists who wear name brand clothes. As a result, they become fascinated and adopt these individuals as their heroes; they also spend large sums of money trying to keep up with the fashion. It is unfortunate to state that ministers are no longer labeled as the elite role models in the community—or as the person that "everyone wants to be like!" At this time, the delinquent desires to be like the one who has the most money and fame, and American teens have been fascinated with outside heroes who gain money and fame without being cowed by societal structures. There have been many debates as to whether hip-hop's attractiveness transcends rebellion among teenagers. If you think about it, everyone needs a sense of belonging!

Juvenile delinquency develops when one is searching for support. However, their pursuit of support is as normal, in comparison, as other adolescents in society. Many adults don't understand the juvenile's burning desire to have a sense of belonging. The human likes to be comforted and shown that they are loved and wanted in a world that creates confusion on a daily basis. As we are present in a new millennium, parental guardians and social service professionals should devote quality time to understanding today's generation and being authentic in their interactions with adolescents. Juveniles want to know that workers are being real or "keeping it real." If they sense that you can't relate to them, they will not give you the time of day, and one will not be able to win them over to the right side!

There are many of us who take for granted the things we learned from our parents. We assume these young people know the difference between right and wrong. However, for many who have experienced trauma, the wrong eventually becomes right. Our society opposes them, punishes them, and gives up on them. There are many juvenile delinquents who are influenced by other factors. For example, many of today's television shows present violence and hatred. I am a firm believer that association develops into assimilation. I know you're probably wondering what I'm talking about, but let me explain what this means. It is simple: if a person hangs around a certain group of people who participate in specific types of behavior, that same individual will eventually engage in the behavioral patterns of that group. For example, Karen was raised in a home where her parents did not use drugs or drink alcohol. However, when Karen went to high school, her peers used both drugs and drank alcohol daily. Karen began to hang around these individuals, whom she classified as her friends, and eventually assimilated the behavior of this group. This type of behavior can also be known as peer pressure.

Adolescents believe that inappropriate behavior has become accepted as a norm in everyday life. It is now viewed as typical, day-to-day living and has become the norm within the world of the adolescent. Unfortunately, the negative atmosphere has intensified for an adolescent. In understanding today's youths, one should be willing to accept that juvenile delinquency stems from many variables. These variables are developed from years of dysfunctional growth that contributes to the overall status of the delinquent.

I always wanted to know why the KKK had so much hate and anger towards people of minority ethnicity until one day, the Lord gave me a revelation regarding the unhealthiness of this cult. Are you ready? Klan members do not just develop this hate overnight. This hatred is imparted from an early age, even from the point when they are in their mother's womb. During this stage, they are being read and taught the doctrine of hate and anger towards minorities and anyone who holds a different view from their own. The ironic thing about the Klan is that they think their doctrine has biblical roots. If you think about it, the juvenile also believes that his or her views are doctrine and should be worshipped and praised by every adolescent and adult. As with most juvenile delinquents, their mental status takes years to influence them to participate in negative activity! According to research, the empirical studies of at-risk samples repeatedly show that children from single-parent families or stepfamilies are more likely to become delinquent than those from two-parent families. This will be discussed more a little later.

Satan's intention to bring division to the home can cause great damage to an adolescent who is being raised in a single-parent home. In this situation, the adolescent is forced to acquire a substitute for the lack of a parent in the family. As a result, the juvenile delinquent behaviors are developed because the adolescent begins to experiment and search for happiness. However, they eventually become deceived by Satan's version of love.

Satan has corrupted the concept of love and has placed in the mind of the delinquent the idea that that they can be saturated in love only through their involvement with illegal acts. The two illegal acts I will discuss entail the illegal act of violating the law of the land and violating the law of God. The delinquent violates the law of the land when they don't comply with the statutes that govern society and, most importantly, statutes pertaining to the Kingdom of God. In essence, natural and spiritual laws are established to bring order to a body of people. Therefore, we are redeemed from the law of the land and must comply with the law of the Kingdom of God. In addition, in complying with God's law (commandments), we will not violate the natural law but will bring glory and honor to the spiritual law of our Savior and Lord Jesus Christ!

The eyes of the delinquent are blinded as Apostle Paul indicated to the church at Corinth, *"whose minds the god of this age has blinded, who do not believe" (2 Corinthians 4:4)*. As a result, the delinquent brings violation to both the natural and spiritual law that has been ordered by God's wisdom and Spirit.

Drugs are another contribution to the overall status of a juvenile delinquent. Juvenile delinquents find the drug business an attractive lifestyle. Juveniles believe that they have a sense of belonging when associated with the drug-dealing environment. It is known that the drug subculture provides a feeling of excitement revolving around the experiences of hustling, as well as the ripping and running life. Society paints the photo that drug sales and use are more prevalent among certain ethnic groups and cultures. However, this is not the truth. I have worked extensively with many cultures and ethnic groups regarding the demonic influence of drugs. Satan is not concerned about the color, but he is concerned about the soul! The drug dealer is not concerned about the soul, but he is concerned about the monetary benefits! If you think about it, Satan is using both the dealer and user. If no intervention is made, they both lose their souls to Satan. There are some youths that believe the drug business to be a risky but profitable way to meet their material and status needs without having to compete on the basis of formal education and job skills.

Many of our adolescents today are given just about everything that they want without having to work for it. Parents today believe that they are doing the best for their child by giving them everything they desire. This parental method creates a monster adolescent that eventually turns into a monster adult if not corrected. Children should not have to be rewarded for good behavior; they should demonstrate good behavior because it's the right thing to do! I am not advocating for a lack of positive reinforcement with your child when they do something positive. However, I *am* advocating for distributing love to your child more than gifts! The greatest gift that one can distribute to their adolescent is love. The gift of love has already been paid for when Jesus Christ died on the cross for our sins. Adolescents need to comprehend the concept of love more than grasping the concept of material things. *"While we do not look at the things which are seen, but at the things which are not seen. For the things which are seen are temporary; but the things which are not seen are eternal" (2 Corinthians 4:18).*

In handling today's youths, one must not be oblivious to their sensitivity or emotional needs. For example, Chris, a youth from a Latino hood in South Central L.A., stated, "I really wanted to meet kids my age, but my dad's restrictions prevented me. I was very lonely and had so much pain in my life. It made me feel important to have my name on walls. The fear and risk of tagging numbed the pain of loneliness" (Tapia, 1995, p. 2).

It is obvious that many adolescents are searching for something to fill the void in their life. There are many parents and loved ones who are unable to identify the unfulfilled area in their son or daughter's life. This is mainly because they encountered the same experiences in their adolescent stage. Parents must be set spiritually free before they can make an impact on their children or loved ones. When the Lord delivered Paul and Silas out of prison, the keeper of the prison asked what must be done to be saved, and they said, *"Believe on the Lord Jesus Christ, and you will be saved, you and your household. Then they spoke the word of the Lord to him and to all who were in the house. And he took them the same hour of the night, and washed their stripes. And immediately he and all his family were baptized (Acts 16:31–33).*

It would be appropriate to state that parental figures play a significant role in the lives of the adolescent, as we so often hear the cliché, "He is a chip from the rock." This cliché can be perceived optimistically or pessimistically. If parental figures are conforming to the commandments of the Lord, the results will be positive. The book of Proverbs states, *"Train up a child in the way he should go, and when he is old, he will not depart from it"* (Proverbs 22:6). When adults are not trained up in the Word of God, it is hard to expect their children to be "perfect children" and compliant to their rules and regulations. We must not be forgetful that children are a product of their environment. Environment is known as the totality of conditions and circumstances affecting growth or development on the existing surroundings that affect an activity. This definition must not be taken lightly; however, the environment plays a prominent part on the total effect of an individual. For example, Potiphar's wife wanted Joseph to be with her, and the more that Joseph refused, the more persistent Potiphar's wife was. *"But it happened about this time, when Joseph went into the house to do his work, and none of the men of the house was inside, that she caught him by his garment, saying, "Lie with me." But he left his garment in her hand, and fled and ran outside"* (Genesis 39:11–12).

The objective of this scripture is to present biblical evidence that the environment can have an effect on an individual. Although Joseph was a faithful and vibrant servant of God, he was placed in an uncomfortable situation. If one would review

Joseph's history, they would see that Joseph was trained in the Word by his father Jacob and obtained a special spiritual character. Joseph may have been affected by the allegations made by Potiphar's wife, but he still remained as a product of his environment. I am simply saying that when an individual is trained in the Word of God, circumstances or crisis can't change the character of the person. However, training individuals to deal with certain situations, or circumstances, equips one for battle and serves as a protection against eternal destruction from the adversary!

> *Stand therefore, having girded your waist with truth, having put on the breastplate of righteousness, and having shod your feet with the preparation of the gospel of peace; above all, taking the shield of faith, with which you will be able to quench all the fiery darts of the wicked. And take the helmet of salvation, and the sword of the Spirit, which is the word of God. (Ephesians 6:14-17)*

In exploring today's generation among adolescents, adults must be open to the acceptance of change. Being able to accept the change in today's generation plays a big role in understanding adolescents. It is sometimes very difficult for adults to stray away from their traditions, upbringing, and culture in the "right way."

If we observe the purpose of a tutor, one will see more clearly what is being explained. A tutor is assigned to assist someone with a particular subject that one has a difficult time understanding. Therefore, it's important for the tutor to break down the material to the very last compound. This may mean the difference between oranges and apples. Well, if we apply this analogy to understanding youth, we can understand that we have to adjust to their level. In ministerial terms, step down from the pulpit! Let's hear what the Holy Spirit says through Apostle Paul in I Corinthians.

> *For though I am free from all men, I have made myself a servant to all, that I might win the more; and to the Jews I became as a Jew, that I might win Jews; to those who are under the law, as under the law, that I might win those who are under the law; to those who are without law, as*

without law (not being without law toward God, but under law toward Christ), that I might win those who are without law; to the weak I became as weak, that I might win the weak. I have become all things to all men, that I might by all means save some (Corinthians 9:19–23).

During this segment of the book, we discussed the generational period in which adolescents are living today. Let us dive a little deeper and observe the root of the term "generation." The Webster's dictionary defines generation as: 1) the act or process of generating; 2) a group of individuals having a common ancestor and constituting a single stage of descent; 3) the average time interval between the birth of parents and the birth of their offspring. In fact, these definitions are very thorough concerning the term "generation." Now, let's look a little closer at the biblical root of "generation." According to the book of Psalms, *"I will make your name to be remembered in all generations; Therefore the people shall praise you forever and ever" (Psalm 45:17).* This scripture verse is stating that the psalmist is advocating for the Lord's name to be remembered in all generations and to be praised by the people forever. One can see that the Lord Jesus Christ is omnipresent (all present), and He was there in the beginning and is present forever. Therefore, He deserves the ultimate praises. After all, everyone must acknowledge His omnipotence one day!

That at the name of Jesus, every knee should bow, of those in heaven, and of those on earth, and of those under the earth, and that every tongue should confess that Jesus Christ is Lord, to the glory of God the Father. (Philippians 2:10–11)

The question I must pose to you is: what god are adolescents bowing down to in this generation? As Christians, we know the history of some of the early Israelites—how some of them worshipped graven images, such as the god of Ashtoreth (goddess of the moon), Remphan (idol worshipped by Israel in the wilderness), Nehushtan (bronze serpent-idol), and many other pagan gods of Mesopotamia, Egypt, and Canaan. Let's look at what the Israelites did in the book of Exodus when Moses was on the mount with the Lord.

7

Now when the people saw that Moses delayed coming down from the mountain, the people gathered together to Aaron, and said to him, "Come, make us gods that shall go before us; for as for this Moses, the man who brought us up out of the land of Egypt, we do not know what has become of him. (Exodus 32:1)

The Bible clearly states that the people gave Aaron golden earrings that were made into a golden calf and worshipped. If we look at our adolescents today, we can see that they also have graven images and false gods that they are worshipping in place of Jesus Christ. Adolescents are worshipping cars, jewelry, celebrities, premarital sex, pornography, egotistical mentalities, drugs, alcohol, dance clubs, demonic home entertainment, as well as fashion styles. These graven images that exist in today's generation are negatively encouraging juvenile delinquency and other forms of immorality. Adolescents must convert to the beginning of all generations.

It is essential that those who work with juveniles on the ministerial basis help them to understand that there is one true, eternal celebrity—Jesus Christ our Lord! Let us now explore more closely the **Juvenile Status in Urban United States** and examine the effects of juvenile delinquency in our urban communities.

CHAPTER 2
JUVENILE STATUS IN URBAN U.S.

There are a number of perceptions and misconceptions about the urban environment throughout the country. There are some individuals who are limited in knowledge in regards to the urban area. Many questions may arise when it concerns observing the relationship between the urban environment and the subject juvenile delinquency. The first thing I would like to accomplish prior to observing urbanization is to first define what urban means. The Webster's dictionary defines urban as: 1) of, pertaining to, or constituting a city and 2) typical of the city or city life.

It is known that citizen killings are due to a variety of societal and interpersonal forces such as urban blight, family deterioration, segregation, poverty, and income inequality, which are well beyond the control of the police. Let's reflect on what the scriptures present about environment violence. Let's examine the book of Genesis.

> *Then the Lord saw the wickedness of man was great in the earth, and that every intent of thoughts of his heart was only evil continually. And the Lord was sorry that He had made man on the earth, and He was grieved in His heart. The earth also was corrupt before God, and the earth was filled with violence. (Genesis 6:5, 6, 11,)*

One can see that violence has been prevented on this earth for an extensive period of time. Just imagine the earth during that time, full of violence and wickedness to the extent that it repented the Lord that He made man on earth and grieved his heart. We must thank God that His mercy endures forever!

A study was conducted to analyze the influence of gender, ethnicity, and grade level on the association between violence exposure and teenagers internalizing and externalizing symptoms and behavior. The persistence of such relationships over time was also examined. Results indicated that violence exposure was correlated with externalizing behavior and internalizing symptoms. Findings also showed high levels of violence exposure for urban youths and association with a range of psychiatric symptoms and indications of poor adjustment regarding the adolescent.

It is quite obvious that our secular society places a lot of emphasis on what they believe to be the cause of urban violence among juveniles. However, Christians seem to obtain great insight regarding the causality of violence. The Bible clearly states that our warfare is not flesh oriented but spiritual! *"For we do not wrestle against flesh and blood, but against principalities, against powers, against the rulers of the darkness of this age, against spiritual host of wickedness in the heavenly places" (Ephesians 6:12).*

Now, let us look at the historical aspects of urbanization. According to research, in 1870, 80 percent of black Americans lived in the rural south; by 1970, 80 percent of black Americans resided in urban locales, half in the north and west. It is also known that World War I had an effect on the urban community.

The outbreak of World War I in 1914 simultaneously increased the demand for U.S. industrial production and reduced the availability of European immigrants to work in northern factories. Between 1910 and 1920, over 500,000 African Americans left their original homes in the south and decided to move to the north. When blacks left the rural south, they primarily moved to major cities like New York, New Jersey, Chicago, Los Angeles, Philadelphia, Michigan, as well as other northern, mid-western, and western urban areas. In addition, as racial diversity increased outside of the south, racial tension also escalated.

Unfortunately, it was a matter of time before crime became prevalent in the urban community. The baby-boom demographic increase in the numbers of socially disconnected youths attained a "critical mass" sufficient to amplify increases in crime. As a result of the black migration, "urban" became equivalent to "black" in the minds of many individuals. Unfortunately, this mentality still exists today among many individuals.

Many urban criminologists have reason to believe that large

cities in particular promote the social conditions leading to crime. It is obvious that from a theological perspective, crime can be classified as a sin. Any time a Christian has violated the law, they have created a sin. The Lord clearly states in His Word that Christians must *"render therefore to Caesar the things that are Caesar's, and to God the things that are God's" (Matthew 22:21).*

For example, Johnny enjoys driving his Porsche on the highway. Although the sign clearly states that the speed limit is 65 mph, he drives 110 mph. According to this scenario, Johnny has sinned against God because he broke the law willingly. Although Christians are saved by grace, it's important that we remain compliant to the laws of society (as discussed in the previous chapter).

It would be appropriate to state that juvenile delinquents have a problem being obedient to rules and regulations and, ultimately, a problem being obedient to God. There are many factors involved with why these behaviors occur continuously in the urban community. This will be elaborated on as the book proceeds; however, the composite picture of the urban criminal is complex. Data indicates that most of the criminals are males. Research shows they are mostly young and although a disproportionate number of property crimes may be committed by a relatively small number of older criminals, many crimes are committed by young men expressing uncontrolled, emotional drives. This is particularly true of crimes of violence.

Urban crime has played a role in multiple decades of the 19th century. It appears to be that the more populated the city area, the more opportunity for crime among juveniles. In regards to juveniles, many offenders seem to return to the same criminal play they initially engaged in. This level of recidivism could be for a number of reasons. As a result, the poor urban minority offender is usually removed to a secure facility, where he stays untreated, with no spiritual and natural assistance, and is ultimately returned to the streets to work for the adversary.

There are many professionals, parents, offenders, and victims who have different perspectives about the juvenile delinquents' urban court system. There are some who actually feel that the court system does justice, and there are those who believe that the courts perform an injustice to individuals and society. For the most part, large cities have large, highly specialized courts and smaller cities tend to have smaller courts, which are shared with the surrounding countryside. The courts operating in cities are usually called state courts because they are governed by state law. A city cannot create its own court system, nevertheless, they are anchored in local politics and tradition, and they are often closely linked to urban politics.

It is necessary to state that the structure of the juvenile court varies from jurisdiction to jurisdiction. Special and separate juvenile courts in certain urban areas devote their total effort to the legal problems of children. Juvenile delinquents in smaller cities and rural areas are often tried by judges from the adult court system. A separate court is organized statewide in several states, and only juvenile judges sit on cases in the various districts of those particular states. In other states, exclusively family court judges who hear both juvenile and domestic related cases handle juvenile offenders.

The judges in the juvenile justice system are overwhelmed by the amount of juvenile cases they experience on a daily basis. In many cases, they find their job to be challenging. The judges are not the only significant role figures in the juvenile court system. The two other prominent figures in the court system are the defense attorney and the prosecutor. The defense attorneys have at least three roles to choose from: 1) an advocate for the child; 2) a guardian or parent surrogate to the child; or 3) an assistant to the court with responsibilities and duties to children. There is evidence to state that juveniles who had counsel received harsher dispositions than those without counsel when present in the court of law. This finding may indicate that juvenile judges are punishing those youths who choose to be represented by counsel.

The prosecutor also has a prominent role in the court system. The prosecutor is entrusted with the dual responsibilities of protecting society and ensuring that children appearing before the court are provided with their basic constitutional rights. Prosecutors are increasingly involved in juvenile court proceedings. However, urban courts operate in a slightly different manner. In urban courts, prosecutors are typically involved in every stage of the proceedings, from intake and detention through disposition. Prosecutors are especially involved in deciding whether juveniles should be waived to the adult court or whether they should be kept in the juvenile court system. In most situations, this makes a big difference. In states where certain offenses are excluded from juvenile court jurisdiction, prosecutors play the role of sending juveniles who commit these offenses to the adult court system.

The following points that will be discussed in this chapter include whether violent juvenile criminals should be treated as adults. There appear to be a number of individuals who think that juvenile criminals should be tried as an adult if they commit an adult crime. However, there are other individuals who believe that juveniles should be tried as a juvenile regardless of what nature the crime entails. Let us explore these two debating perspectives held by society.

> Violent crimes by youths, such as the 1998 school shooting in Jonesboro, Arkansas, in which four students and one teacher were killed, point to a need to treat some juvenile criminals as adults, argues Linda J. Collier in the following viewpoint. She asserts that the juvenile justice system is outdated because it was designed to deal with the vandals and petty thieves of an earlier era, not today's juvenile murderers and rapists. The state should set a uniform minimum age for trying violent youths as adults. (Hurley, 1999, p. 64)

It is not a new or unusual phenomenon for children to commit violent crimes at younger ages. Why is this? The adversary realizes that he has a short period of time to do his dirty work by corrupting the minds and souls of God's children. Therefore, the evil forces have increased in all dimensions of life. Juveniles now are more likely to be the perpetrators of serious and deadly crimes such as arson, aggravated assault, rape, and murder. Governmental statistics, since 1965, show that the number of twelve-year-olds arrested for violent crimes has doubled and the number of thirteen- and fourteen-year-olds has tripled. In many states, changes in the juvenile crime laws have lowered the age at which a juvenile can be tried as an adult for certain crimes. Although the majority of states allow juveniles to be tried as adults, it varies according to jurisdiction, judicial circuit, state, and judge.

If one would reflect on the Old Testament laws (Deuteronomic Code), one would see that these laws were an expression of what the Lord mandated for His children. Let's look a little closer to Old Testament laws. According to biblical research, there are eight distinct categories of civil law in the Old Testament: 1) laws regulating leaders, 2) laws regulating the army, 3) laws respecting criminals, 4) laws dealing with crimes against property, 5) laws relating to human treatment, 6) laws about person and family rights, 7) laws about property rights, and 8) laws regulating other social behavior (Youngblood, 1989, p. 748). An interesting thing about these laws was that God always gave one an opportunity to benefit from His grace. Let's examine the laws against criminals. According to the third category of civil law against criminal offenses, God defined what a criminal offense is and what the proper punishment for each offense was to be. Biblical research supports that all crimes were sins or offenses against God's law. Since there were degrees of punishments, there were also degrees of sin under the law. God prohibited the Israelites from punishing criminals excessively. Let us look at a scripture from the book of Deuteronomy.

If there is a dispute between men, and they come to court, that the judges may judge them, and they justify the righteous and condemn the wicked, *"then it shall be, if the wicked man deserves to be beaten, that the judge will cause him to lie down and be beaten in his presence, according to his guilt, with a certain number of blows. Forty blows he may give him and no more, lest he should exceed this and beat him with many blows above these, and your brother be humiliated in your sight,* (Deuteronomy 25:1–3).

Most people would say that the laws in the Old Testament were quite stringent. The offenders were given a fair trial whenever they violated the law. Judges were charged not to be partial in favor of the rich or against the poor, widows, aliens, or others who might be helpless. However, they were to listen to the witnesses meticulously, examine the evidence, and make decisions on the basis of what God had revealed in his written law. In addition, they also presided over making or nullifying all contracts. It would be appropriate to state that regardless of whether juvenile delinquents are tried as an adult or as a minor, the problem remains and is usually addressed in a legal channel. The parents, church, professionals, and the community must do what they can to help prevent adolescents from conforming to the system of juvenile delinquency.

As Christians, it is in our power to stop the devil in his tracks. The difficult thing is that many Christians don't realize the power that was given to them by the Lord. Jesus said to His disciples, *"Behold, I give you the authority to trample on serpents and scorpions, and over all the power of the enemy: and nothing shall by any means hurt you"* *(Luke 10:19).* The Christian has the same power that Christ demonstrated during His ministry on earth. I know this may be hard for some to believe; however, this is the whole truth and nothing but the truth! Christians have the power in Jesus' name to command Satan to stop bringing havoc to their homes, relationships, finances, and other areas of Christian life. If your adolescent is displaying delinquent symptoms, pray as if you have never prayed before, and even start a prayer group with strong Christian friends, relatives, and church members.

As a child growing up, I recall listening to a secular song that can relate to what we are discussing at this time. The title of the song was, "I got the power." We have to show this devil that we have the power and stand firm on what Jesus said in His Word! *"All authority has been given to me in heaven and on earth"* *(Matthew 28:18).*

CHAPTER 3
POLITICAL & ECONOMIC CONCERNS

The relationship of community poverty to the level of violence against children within a community has been the source of much research and debate.

There are those individuals who believe that economic and political concerns are not relevant to the actual causes of juvenile delinquency. However, there are those who believe that politics and economics have everything to do with juvenile delinquency. The focus of this chapter is to explore the effects of politics and economics as it pertains to juvenile delinquency and bring out biblical explanations regarding these effects. A substantial body of research over the past forty years has established links between violent crime, poverty, and related phenomena such as low socioeconomic status (SES) and unemployment. It is known that the unemployment rate and level of income inequality are associated positively and significantly with justifiable homicide rates for blacks. Poverty is not the only cause of significant negative impact on such killings. This may be shocking to individuals who have held this view to thy kingdom come! ☺ The bottom line is that people need Jesus! Jesus will never instruct anyone to engage in crime due to food shortage or any other reason because He is the provider. Many secular researchers believe that the economy and unemployment are a complex problem:

> The problem of America's inner cities has never seemed more pressing or more hopelessly complex. Persistent poverty, overcrowding, underemployment, substandard housing, and

physical deterioration of inner cities are stubborn facts. Urban riots act to call public attention to these conditions again and again for most of America. The cities have come to be seen as a kaleidoscope of social services for the threatened and threatening urban population. (Woodson, 1981, p. 2)

There appears to be a number of variables on the causes of juvenile delinquency based on the perspective of some researchers. The rates of violent crime and juvenile delinquency in many communities are highly linked with impoverishment. In the early years, children worked as long as their parents, when work was available. Prior to 1850, overproduction and speculation in both England and America generated great economic depression and the rates of welfare and vagrancy escalated.

For working class boys forced into the streets due to unemployment and overcrowded domestic households, inadequate and illegal employment such as prostitution and robbery had a strong hold on them.

As U.S. citizens and residents, we must not be naïve enough to believe that economic challenges only affect individuals within the American culture. The subject of unemployment obtains an international prevalence and scope. There are immigrants who have also encountered difficult experiences as well. The reliance on one's "own people" was a response to shared adversities. Immigrant families encountered a wealth of problems, including the language barrier, difficulties in obtaining employment, low income, and trouble finding housing. They faced the possibility of losing their own customs and values to American ways. In many cases, this still remains the same today. It's difficult for one to change the way they have always done something!

Because there seems to be this great financial challenge in certain communities, many adolescents (juvenile delinquents) conform to drug sales as an easy method to acquire finances. Some youths perceive the drug business as a risky but profitable way to meet their material and station needs without having to compete on the basis of formal education and job skills. Drug use in this country is pervasive among young people. Beer and marijuana meet these criteria better than many hard drugs.

18

Availability and potency are also important in drug use for these substances are likely to be used as means to other ends, mostly for achieving excitement. For example, marijuana, alcohol, and other drugs used at football games, concerts, parties, outings, dances, and similar activities add to the excitement already inherent in such activities or, in some cases, produce excitement when it may appear to be lacking.

Before we elaborate on the topic of drugs, let us explore the concept of money and the role that money played in the Old Testament. Money came into existence when ancient people stopped living the lives of hunters and farmers. Money in the Old Testament times was also known as the barter system. Grain, oil, and wine were also used in bartering. Spices were also a gift that was offered by the Queen of Sheba to Solomon. Gradually, as communities became more organized, tradesmen traveled between these settlements. Products were distributed from one region to another. It was a matter of time before metals began to replace goods and services as items of exchange. The need for bronze and copper increased for use in weapons production, farming tools, and for offerings. The early Egyptians, Semites, and Hitites shaped gold and silver into rings, bars, or rounded nodules for easier trading efforts. It was known that the children of Jacob used sundries of money that possibly could have been metal rings twined together with strings.

One can see that money in the early ages was for buying and exchange, a practice that continues today. There are many juvenile delinquents that engage in drug sales because they have a spirit for the love of money. The Bible clearly states *"for the love of money is a root of all kinds of evil: for which some have strayed from the faith in their greediness, and pierced themselves through with many sorrows"* (I Timothy 6:10).

The Old Testament book of Joshua presents an example pertaining to the love of money. When Joshua was in leadership over the Israelites, he instructed them to acquire from Jericho the silver, gold, and vessels of brass and iron and to place them into the treasury of the Lord. Unfortunately, not every Israelite was compliant to this instruction. Achan took two hundred shekels of silver and a wedge of gold of fifty shekels in weight and hid them under his tent. The disobedience of Achan caused major consequences to him and his family. (Joshua 7:24–25)

One can see that money can be utilized for many adequate purposes, but one can have the wrong motive for desiring money. Achan's desire for money was solely out of greed, which led to his destruction and the destruction of his entire family. If one would apply this Old Testament example to juvenile delinquents today, one would conclude that many juveniles are also experiencing a love for money. This love of money has controlled their lives and has caused many of them to stray from their purpose in life. *"For what profit is it to a man if he gains the whole world, and loses his own soul? Or what will a man give in exchange for his soul"* (Matthew 16:26).

It would be appropriate to state that employment in today's society is a necessity, but it can create multiple problems when it becomes the center or cornerstone of one's life.

As we discussed earlier, drug dealing can eventually turn into something greater. Concurrent research on Miami delinquents and Tampa "high risk" youths support the conclusion that involvement in drug dealing places individuals at high risk of becoming users themselves. Drug abuse among adolescents has increased dramatically and has become a major issue within the adolescent population. There are some professionals who believe that Congress had a lot to do with the drug enhancement within the U.S. As discussed earlier, the adversary is the one who is behind this drug corruption. Statistics show that Congress is serious about their responsibility to represent their constituents in Washington, securing $13 billion annually on drug control programs. The result: drug abuse is rising dramatically among our youth. It is obvious that the $13 billion that is allocated to drug programs is not doing an adequate job of preventing adolescents from using drugs. Why is this? The answer to this question is that many of these programs are not Christian based. It takes an act of deliverance in order to stop someone from using drugs!

Drugs can cause someone to be in bondage for many years. I can recall counseling a client that mentioned his dependence on crack for ten years. The young adult was an engineer in California who made over $120,000 dollars a year. I was astonished when he told me his age because he looked about fifteen years older than what he mentioned. He spent his money on crack every time he received a paycheck. He mentioned that he had a house, a vehicle, and financially lived beyond the average American with plenty left over. Unfortunately, he lost it all to crack. As the young man begun to proceed in his conversation, he began to cry in a very intense manner. It was a hopeless and helpless cry, as though he could never be delivered from this attack of Satan. I acknowledged that there were only select moments when I could talk about Jesus in the secular community, primarily whenever a client brings up God. The magnificent thing that occurred was that he did bring up the Lord and how he was a faithful Christian but had backslid. I began to talk about God's security in salvation and His unconditional love, which He offers every individual that walks upon this earth! I told him that he could recommit his life to the Lord free of charge because Jesus paid the price for him, as well as for the world. The client began to feel encouraged, and I prayed with him to restore his relationship with the Lord. His ultimate deliverance depended on how bad he wanted it!

During the last few years, the use of illegal drugs has increased 50 percent. Criminologists believe that the use of drugs increase the likelihood that a youth will be arrested and referred to the juvenile justice system. Other short-term consequences include the vulnerability to using other drugs, loss of interest in school, and impaired psychological functioning. One of Satan's strategies is to paint an attractive picture so that one can purchase it at any price! Satan is trying the same old tricks that he used during the ministry of our Lord Jesus Christ. Jesus confronted Satan on three occasions when the Spirit led Him into the wilderness after fasting forty days and nights. The Bible tells us that Satan took Jesus into the holy city and set Him on the pinnacle of the temple and tempted Jesus. *"Then the devil left Him, and behold, angels came and ministered to Him" (Matthew 4:11).* Fortunately for us, Jesus never accepted the devil's offer. It did not matter how pretty the picture was that Satan painted for Jesus because it all belongs to Jesus anyway! The lesson to learn in this true story (as well as other lessons) is that Jesus combated Satan with the Word of God. It is only the Word of God that can put a stop to a specific attack designed by the enemy. Christian believers must be able to teach the delinquent the power of God. Although the enemy will be in constant pursuit, show them the weapon, which is the gospel of Jesus Christ!

As we stated earlier in this chapter, there are many variables that pertain to juvenile delinquency. Let's explore the socioeconomic factors that affect juvenile delinquency. The American social class structure has come under increased scrutiny over the past decade. Notorious headlines such as "the rich get richer" and "income disparity between the rich and poor increases" are frequently found in the media.

Media headlines reflect statistics indicating that a rather small percentage (20 percent) of the population controls more than 86 percent of the wealth in the nation and receives more than 45 percent of the income. In addition, the lower 20 percent of the population controls less than 1 percent of the wealth and receives less than 5 percent of the income. The gap between the bottom 20 percent and the top 20 percent is increasing. It appears true that the socio-economic climate can cause diversity in the black community. There is also a large diversity in the black societal section that affects the developmental experiences of black adolescents.

It is necessary that the socio-economic status and individual family structures of blacks should be recognized in developing intervention programs, especially when it pertains to teenage pregnancy. However, these programs will be highlighted more clearly when we get more direct with the Divine Intervention among juvenile delinquents. The social and economic changes that separated work from the home also fostered a newer conception within the urban middle class of the family as a "domestic haven." This innovative vision of childhood led parents and others to differentiate and isolate children from adults. As the traditional networks of families, churches, and communities fatigued, luxury organizations played increasing roles in maintaining social control, social welfare, and fostering the vision of the population.

The socio-economical system existing in the criminal environment didn't appear instantaneously. The first half of the 19th century experienced demographic social and economic changes that were threatening. Cohesion and stability began to alter the social construction of youth. It wasn't until "the separation of work from the home" that social roles and economic values relative to children and their mothers were altered. The modern social construction of childhood excluded children from the world of work, reduced their economic contributions, prolonged their dependencies, and resulted in greater responsibilities on their parents and guardians. The separation of work from the home also made contributions to the segregation of sexes and the relegation of women mainly to the domestic sphere. The family became a unit of usage rather than of production; urban, middle-class fathers worked outside the home and women remained at home and assumed both domestic and child rearing responsibilities.

Unfortunately, this isn't the same experience among juveniles who endure poverty. The social science council believes that people are poor because they are deprived of opportunities, comforts, and self-respect regarded as normal in the community to which they belong. There are those that argue that "relative" poverty (or economic inequity), not absolute poverty, is a more relevant variable for explaining a real variation in criminal activity. The assessment of the relationship between a neighborhood's economic activities must consider other variables that may have some association with the broad distribution of crime. These may include 1) residential mobility, 2) racial integration, 3) neighborhood desegregation, 4) household composition and family structure, and 5) population density. Many of these variables are viewed as important because of their potential association in regards to levels of social control.

As a young Christian growing up, I can recall many moments when I meditated on doing something that was not necessarily the 100% right thing to do. I then asked myself, what would Jesus do? Adolescents must come to the point where they compare their premeditated acts with the righteous acts that the Lord endeavored. Race and ethnicity, or economic status, should have no significance at all when it pertains to doing the right thing! It's been too long that we have heard the excuse of an adolescent not holistically doing well because they are struggling financially and lack financial assistance.

Research also supports that violent crime rates are significantly lower in areas that are more socially integrated. It also seems that violent crime rates are higher in areas that are more densely populated or characterized by greater residential instability. The ecology has continually presented a connection between severely declining urban neighborhoods and rates of delinquency. In addition, the deteriorated residential areas generally have the highest crime and delinquency rates. It is known that neighborhoods labeled by high levels of crime and delinquency over a time span of several decades may be considered lost for purposes of effective crime reduction. Here, one can see that society is sometimes easy to surrender and give up on the delinquent and certain residential areas that are highly populated in crime associated with juvenile delinquents. The proper manner to address crime is spiritually! In order for juvenile delinquency to be reduced, the Spirit of the Lord must be present. The ministerial community should unite their efforts in order to have a great impact and bring destruction to Satan's kingdom. They must "rise up" a generation of righteous youths who will one day become our spiritual leaders.

It appears that the underclass typically feels excluded from society, rejects commonly accepted values, suffers from behavioral as well as income deficiencies, and is increasingly trapped in the context of poverty from one generation to the next. The extremely high rates of property, drug, and violent crimes, as well as poor individuals and groups, are likely to be jobless and welfare dependent.

In the New Testament, Corinth was considered the connecting link between Rome and was the capital of the world and the east. It was a city that was known for gambling, legalized temple prostitution, as well as for bronze, pottery, and shipbuilding. Biblical research indicates that upon Apostle Paul's arrival, approximately 500,000 people lived at Corinth, including merchants, sailors, athletes, as well as slaves (sometimes freed but with no place to go). This was the population of people who eventually made up the Corinthian church. They had to learn to live together in harmony, although their national, social, economic, and religious backgrounds were different.

In the book of Acts, we read about the angel of the Lord instructing Philip to go south to Gaza. In obedience to the Lord's instructions, Philip arose and went and saw an Ethiopian Eunuch (a eunuch of great authority under Candance Queen of the Ethiopians). The scripture states that this eunuch was sitting on his chariot reading about the prophet Isaiah.

So Philip ran to him, and heard him reading the prophet Isaiah, and said, Do you understand what you are reading? And he said, "How can I, unless someone guides me? And he asked Philip to come and sit with him. Then Philip opened his mouth, and beginning at this scripture, preached Jesus to him. (Acts 8:28–35)

If you think about it, Philip was of a different cultural and economic status than the Ethiopian eunuch, who was in charge of the treasury of the Ethiopian Queen Candance. Nevertheless, this didn't prevent Philip from approaching his chariot. After preaching the mystery of the gospel, Philip baptized him and brought him to the Lord. Therefore, the eunuch was saved by the grace of God and water baptized.

It would be appropriate to state that it's possible for individuals to live together in peace, regardless of religion, ethnicity, race, etc. It is also necessary to state that one of the major problems that people face in their personal lives today is a lack of positive change. This can create or cause spiritual damage in one's life. It causes people to hate and to obtain other unfruitful spirits that are not of God. The children of the world ultimately are affected because of the choices their parents, or guardians, made. Apostle Paul writes in Philippians:

Brethren, I do not count myself to have apprehended; but one thing I do, forgetting those things which are behind and reaching forward to those things which are ahead. I press toward the goal for the prize of the upward call of God in Christ Jesus. (Philippians 3:13–14)

It is obvious that the Lord wants us to forget those negative past experiences and move forward. Here is a poem that the Lord led me to write during a time in my life when the adversary reminded me about my past experiences.

YESTERDAY IS THE PAST

As children of God, it is important for us to acknowledge that yesterday is the past. The traumas and internal detriments of yesterday will not be converted to the life functions of today, if one lives in the past! We must allow our hearts to forgive those who trespass our rights and accept the blessings of tomorrow.

If a blind man is unable to forget the past, it will be quite difficult for him to envision the beauty of today. The riches of life can only be accumulated from maturity and how one enables the history of yesterday to determine their wisdom of today. Yesterday is past!

Allow yesterday's experience to serve as a cornerstone in your future endeavors. As imperfect creatures, we tend to dwell on the events of yesterday and lose focus of the activities of today. If you allow yourself to alleviate the pain of yesterday, today will not end but will be the beginning of a new life!

As a blind man learns to cope with his impairment, he develops strategies to convert his darkness into a candle! As children of God, we should allow Jesus Christ to convey us to the light and remember that yesterday is the past!

Politics and economics play a significant role when it pertains to juvenile delinquency. As partially mentioned before, the neighborhood characteristics (integration), racial heterogeneity, and population density, as well as other factors, can have an adverse effect on young people. Some other risk factors of delinquency include individual characteristics, family, school, and peer group influences. These additional elements will be explored as this book continues, but the above risk factors call on communities to identify and understand what their children are actually exposed to. Communities must enhance protective factors that promote positive behavior, health, well being, and personal success. Effective delinquency prevention efforts must be comprehensive, covering multiple risk factors.

Individuals and Christian community organizations must come into agreement that it's our obligation to ensure that juvenile delinquents (and family members) receive the services that they are not only entitled to but need in order to live a normal life. In order to love our neighbor, it requires accommodating their essential needs. This may mean food, shelter, clothing, and assistance in employment. This also means setting those free from bondage, breaking the yoke of the enemy, and ultimately doing the things that most people don't really want to do.

Christianity is a demonstration of love. In addition, Christians should be willing to give and will one day be accountable for their actions. Jesus says, *"for I was hungry and you gave Me food; I was thirsty and you gave Me drink; I was a stranger and you took Me in; I was naked and you clothed Me; I was sick and you visited Me; I was in prison and you came to Me" (Matthew 25:35–36).*

God expects His children to present a father figure. The next chapter will discuss the significance of a father figure and family unit in the life of a juvenile delinquent.

CHAPTER 4
SIGNIFICANCE OF FATHER FIGURE AND FAMILY UNIT

The significance of a father figure in the life of a juvenile is extremely prominent. Before exploring this prominence, let us first define the word father. According to Webster's dictionary, father is referred to as a male parent, a child's male ancestor, a priest, "God." Yes, in actuality, a father is what God is to those who love Him, and to them who remain in the world. *"For God so loved the world that He gave His only begotten Son, that whoever believes in Him should not perish but have everlasting life"* (*John 3:16*).

It would be appropriate to state that a father gives in order for a child to obtain. One of the biggest problems that juvenile delinquents face today is that they not only lack fathers in the home but they lack father figures as well. Let's see what research supports in this area of study! Bendel (1999) found that "children living in homes where fathers are absent are far more likely to be expelled from or drop out of school, develop emotional or behavioral problems, commit suicide, and fall victim to child abuse or neglect" (p.38). Statistics show that in 1960, fewer than eight million children live in fatherless families. However, the total has risen to nearly twenty-four million. Lack of father figures in the home can cause children to develop into juvenile criminals within the community. Data supports that men who show up without dads currently represent 70 percent of the prison population serving long-term sentences.

Fathers are important for the well being of children; they also represent some level of tradition in families. This helps ensure the continuity of civilization by reproducing the species and socializing children. Most people seem to comprehend the obvious benefits of reproduction, but the important role that parents play in socializing children remains misunderstood and undervalued.

Shockingly, the teen population is expected to grow by 20 percent over the next decade, which is particularly the generation that is likely to be raised without fathers. Based on these statistics, one could see that juvenile delinquency is an epidemic. Let's look at some more current statistics that pertain to children today. Data presents that 7,700 children become sexually active, 1,100 children have abortions, 2,200 children are born out of wedlock, 600 children contract syphilis or gonorrhea, and six children commit suicide daily. Although these statistics occur on a daily basis, they are changing rapidly. It would be appropriate to state that children are born into a world and become very vulnerable to facing direct sin. As a result, it is difficult for children to adapt to morals and ethics when they are victims of a broken home.

Let us first define what a broken home is. Criminologists define "broken home" as the family that has experienced divorce, separation, desertion, or the death of one of the parents. Some of the above elements can lead to a dysfunctional family.

The family has traditionally been viewed as the most important force in the socialization of youth. In addition to giving a child his/her principal identity, the family teaches social rules, moral standards, and society's laws and functional procedures. The failure of the family to accommodate children's emotional, intellectual, and social needs can be one of the most significant factors in their turning point in criminal activity.

Out of all the social institutions that influence the adolescent, family is the most critical and is the foundation of the rest of one's life. Parents become critical role models for their children, and children often begin to see the world through the eyes of their parents and display the same behaviors and thought patterns. For example, Jesus and His disciples were a family. They traveled together, they worked together, bunked together, preached together, cried and marveled together, and most prominently, "broke bread together." Jesus demonstrated what a true family ought to be!

And as they were eating, Jesus took bread, blessed and broke it, and gave it to the disciples and said, "Take, eat;

*this is My body." Then He took the cup, and gave thanks,
and gave it to them, saying, "Drink from it, all of you.
"For this is My blood of the new covenant, which is shed
for many for the remission of sins. (Matthew 26:26–28)*

The interesting thing about the last supper is that Jesus knew who was going to betray Him. In fact, Jesus knew this before the foundation of the world. The love of Jesus still overcame the plans of Satan.

Who could ask for a better father (role model) than Jesus Christ? Jesus loved the delinquent (Judas) who was initially in His family prior to becoming deceived by Satan. This is the kind of love that we should demonstrate in our homes. Christians should remember the fact that they have the victory! Guardians (parents) may be experiencing difficulties with a delinquent child; however, Christians have the victory! Apostle Paul writes in 2 Corinthians, *"We are troubled on every side, yet not distressed. We are perplexed, but not in despair; persecuted, but not forsaken; cast down, but not destroyed; always bearing about in the body the dying of the Lord Jesus, that the life also of Jesus might be made manifest in our body" (2 Cor 4:8–10).*

Many people agree that the family is the first line of defense in dealing with the problem of delinquency, but there are some forms of family life that may be contributing to delinquency rather than solving it. The concept of the "broken home" could be a complex one; the mother and father's presence in the home doesn't necessarily imply that the home is psychologically normal. One critical aspect of being a single parent, which generally refers to a female head of household, is that economic stressors become a variable.

Let us look more closely at the broken homes from which these children come. It is suggested that the earlier the parental break occurs in the developmental history of the child, the greater its impact on the development of delinquency. It seems that younger children experiencing divorce not only have less experience outside the home but also lack the cognitive and social competencies to understand and deal with the dissolution of their parents' marital relationship. It may take some time for a victim to recover from the pain of divorce. A parental divorce may be very painful to a child. It may take some children years to recover from the structural breakup of the family. During this time, the child may exhibit a variety of negative behaviors and attitudes.

Let's look more closely at what a home is. The Webster's dictionary defines home as follows: 1) a place where one lives, residence; 2) an apartment or home; 3) a household; 4) a place of origin; 5) a habitat. If one looks at the term home from a biblical view, he/she can see a relationship with the definition that is provided by Webster's dictionary. As Christians, our home is a dwelling place for the Holy Spirit to live. Christians are people that are created to be filled by the Holy Spirit. Humanity in its physical and spiritual form belongs to the Lord!

> *Or do you not know that your body is the temple of the Holy Spirit who is in you, whom you have from God, and you are not your own? For you were bought at a price; therefore glorify God in your body and in your spirit, which are God's (1 Corinthians 6:19–20).*

If our temple is kept in order, our home will have a much greater chance to sustain. One of the biggest problems that an individual can face is their own self. Humans tend to place the blame on everyone else. It appears difficult for one to examine one's self and then ask the physician to perform surgery.

I Corinthians states: *"But let a man examine himself, and so let him eat of that bread, and drink of that cup" (11:28).* On the contrary, we desire to examine others, although we are not qualified to do so! Jesus made it clear to the disciples not to judge each other. Let's look more closely at what the Word of God says:

> *And why do you look at the speck in your brother's eye, but do not consider the plank in your own eye? Or how can you say to your brother, let me remove the speck from your eye; and look, a plank is in your eye. (Matthew 7:3–4)*

God wants His children to acknowledge the iniquity in themselves before discerning it in one's brother or sister. In order for a home to be placed in order, it must start with the individual and most pertinently, it must begin with the parents. God has given the responsibility to the parents to be custodians for His children. Children are also mandated to obey the godly instructions given by their parents. (Ephesians 6:1–3)

Mothers and fathers engage in parenting differently. Mothers are known to be more verbal, whereas fathers are more physical. Mothers are known to encourage personal safety and caution, whereas fathers are more challenging when it relates to achievement, independence, being self-sufficient, and risk-taking. The fact that mothers and fathers parent differently is not to say that one group does a better job than the other. Children and adolescents need a combination of what mothers and fathers bring to the parenting table in order to obtain good, moral character.

It is obvious that society tends to present evidence that black men are absent from the home. This evidence is accurate in some sense but is being challenged in today's society. There are some African-American fathers who honestly act as a "father" to their children. In many ways, the "invisible man" is making efforts in surfacing from the dung. African-American men are fulfilling the provider-role more each day. African-American fathers see work as a means to an end, such as providing a means to effectively carry out the husband and father roles and its obligations. However, many fathers are finding it challenging to engage in multiple tasks as a father. Many fathers from diverse socioeconomic backgrounds are feeling the pains of the economic recession in the United States. African-American fathers; however, are experiencing greater tension and strife from the problems of the economic situation as they have been historically on less firm economic and occupational standing than other cultures and ethnic groups.

It is necessary to state the difficulties for any single parent to effectively raise children in today's society. Statistics support that "the traditional image of an American family—working father, a housewife, and two school age children—constitutes only 6 percent of U.S. households" (Jensen, 1996, p. 188). It is possible that these economic strains can contribute to the development of a delinquent child. Many parents (mainly single parents) are so occupied with trying to make a living that they don't have sufficient time to devote to their children or spouse. Consequently, children are achieving attention through other activities. For example, it appears that children are emulating many scenes in movies that are destructive, dangerous, and at times deadly to innocent people. It is unfortunate that a child becomes vulnerable to these acts when there is a lack of supervision provided. The facade of civilization is very thin. Any human has the capacity under the right circumstances to behave savagely. Some of us need only a little motivation to do so!

The school, as well as the family and peer group, acts as an important Microsystems in the child's social network. Let's define what a Microsystem is. Microsystems are known as patterns of activities, roles, and interpersonal relations that take place within settings that are directly experienced by an individual. Researchers find that potential dropouts are more likely to be involved in delinquency than their peers who eventually graduate. The school is indicated as the critical social context for the development of delinquent behavior. The adolescents (children) usually find a sense of support, or family, when they attend school. Therefore, it is also considered an environment for criminal activity. For the past few decades, schools have been the settings of vandalism and violence.

It seems that outside the family, the school has the greatest influence in the lives of children and adolescents. It is possible that school can profoundly influence the hopes and dreams of youth. It is evident that there is a correlation between youth crime and inadequate academic behavior. One would say that those who are more likely to become involved in youth crime typically have some educational challenges, have low basic academic skills, are years behind their modal grades in school, tend to be disruptive, and possibly have been dropped or expelled out of school.

In fact, there appears to be a percentage of delinquents who have learning disabilities. Tests in the national delinquency and learning disability study included a three to four-hour session to assess learning disabilities. The results identified thirty-one learning-disabled delinquents.

It is essential to convert to what was discussed initially in this chapter and discuss the significance of the father in the home from a biblical perspective. The concept of family as the "social unit" goes back to creation in the book of Genesis. After God created Adam, God declared, *"It is not good that man should be alone" (Genesis 2:18)*. He created woman and joined her to man and they became *"one flesh" (Genesis 2:24)*. The family was designed by God to provide relation and comfort for the various members of the family. In addition, the institution of marriage was approved and sanctioned by Jesus.

It is God's intentions for the family to be a harmonious unit and that love for God should be the objective of the family. *"You shall love the Lord your God with all your heart, with all your soul, and with all your strength" (Deuteronomy 6:5)*. In actuality, if a couple becomes separated, the entire family is then divided. As Christians, we know that division is not of God but of Satan. Families must be placed upon a rock in order to stand firm. Jesus said to Peter, *"and on this rock I will build My church; and the gates of Hades shall not prevail against it" (Matthew 16:18)*. If families are built on the rock of Jesus Christ, more families will be saved and fewer adolescents would conform to juvenile delinquency.

On the contrary, sometimes adolescents will choose to remain in their inappropriate or delinquent behavior even when their siblings or peers may engage in a more positive direction. For an example, let's look at the story of Cain and Abel.

> *And Adam knew Eve his wife, and she conceived and bore Cain, and said, I have acquired a man from the Lord. Then she bore again, this time his brother Abel. Now Abel was a keeper of sheep, but Cain was a tiller of the ground. And in process of time it came to pass that Cain brought an offering of the fruit of the ground to the Lord. Abel also brought of the firstborn of his flock and of their fat. And the Lord respected Abel and his offering, but he did not respect Cain and his offering. And Cain was very angry? And his countenance fell. (Genesis: 4:1–5)*

As a result of God not respecting Cain's offering, Cain rose up against his brother Abel and killed him. In this biblical example, one can say that Cain suffered consequences for murdering his brother. The Lord said to Cain, *"So now you are cursed from the earth, which has opened its mouth to receive your brother's blood from your hand" (Genesis 4:11)*. Cain was punished because of his inadequate offering to the Lord and violence. He was the oldest son of Adam and Eve, but yet he was also the first murderer.

It was an evil spirit that led Cain to kill his brother, as well as an evil spirit that led Adam and Eve into sin. (Genesis 2:16–17)

It is obvious that Adam and Eve weren't compliant to the commandment that God instructed them to follow. One can see that their decision of disobedience eventually affected their oldest

35

son Cain. In other words, original sin created a generation of sin. In addition, it's the same sin that causes parents to lead their children astray from the Word of God, as well as juvenile delinquents in developing a heartbeat for negative behavior. According to research, there seems to be a decline in traditional families.

> One of the most significant social changes of the past decades has occurred in the types of families and households. Married couple families with children under the age of 18 made up 25 percent of households in 1997, down significantly from 40.3 percent in 1970. In 1970, among families with children, married couple families accounted for 89 percent of families; families headed by mothers, 10 percent; and families headed by fathers, 1 percent. (Begun, 1999, p.13)

It is necessary to conclude that families are being attacked. The family must be spiritually connected and unified. The father must be responsible for the spiritual well being of the family. Theologians suggest that the father functions as the priest of his family, sacrificing on its behalf. For example, Job rose up early in the morning in order to give a burnt offering to the Lord for his family:

> *So it was, when the days of feasting had run their course, that Job would send and sanctify them, and he would rise early in the morning and offer burnt offerings according to the number of them all: for Job said, it may be that my sons have sinned and cursed God in their hearts. Thus Job did regularly. (Job 1:5)*

This scripture is basically saying that the father must fulfill the spiritual role as the head of the home. Job was the head of his home, as well as the spiritual leader and trainer for righteousness. The home can only sustain through spiritual devotions. Satan desires to destroy the home. The scripture states that, *"no weapon that is formed against you shall prosper"* (Isaiah 54:17). The following chapter will discuss material on demonic spirits and how these spirits have a negative effect on juvenile delinquents.

CHAPTER 5
SATANISM AND THE JUVENILE

Satanic oppression is a topic that most community-active individuals hesitate to discuss. Satanism has an effect on a juvenile's criminal activity. First, let us first define what Satanism is. Satanism corrupts accepted moral values and eventually becomes the symptom of a greater problem. Satanic involvement is the result of a troubled youth coming into contact with experienced deviants. The youth then receives the opportunity to learn about deviant behavior through imitation and modeling.

The word Satan is derived from the Hebrew word *Shatan*. In the New Testament, Satan, also known as "the adversary," is referred to by the Greek word *diabolos*. This word can be interpreted as "devil" and carries a meaning as slanderer or tempter. Jesus' temptation in the desert following His baptism can be used as an example of the role diabolos was thought to play, as far as tempting man through his physical nature and persecuting mankind.

Throughout history, Satan is depicted in many different forms, specifically grotesque. In addition, portrayals are found in illustrations from middle age manuscripts and in some paintings. Today, Satan is pictured in a variety of media: album covers, books, paintings, television and movies, as well as other areas. Other research supports that the talk show hosts rely on psychiatric experts to explain the danger to Satanists and to those they might victimize. Satanism can sometimes be misinterpreted as ostentatious: which is defined as a lavish or pretentious display. Ostentation can also be known as the physical re-enactment of local legends. Ironically, the role-playing done on these legend-trips is the significant thing to adolescents, and the legend serves mainly as an excuse to escape adult supervision. They commit antisocial acts and experiment illicitly with both drugs and sex. Satan can also be referred to as the adversary! Satan can be considered as both a rebel and a corrupter. He leads the angels who, according to *2 Peter 2:4 and Jude 6–7*, who will be under restraint in "dungeon" and "chains" and face judgment of eternal fire for their sins *(Matt. 25:41)*. These fallen angels, whose character is set in the mold of their first transgression, as later Adam's would be, are called demons in the New Testament. God restrains them to limit what they can do, but their hostility toward God and the godly has no limits. This beast continues to cause chaos in any way possible.

Satan can also be known as the tempter. For example, Satan tempted Jesus in the wilderness after Jesus was baptized. The prominent lesson behind the temptation is that Jesus overcame it by the Word of God. Satan tempted Jesus three times, but the response of Jesus was the following: [1] *"It is written, man shall not live by bread alone, but by every word that proceeds from the mouth of God,"* [2] *"It is written again, you shall not tempt the Lord your God,"* [3] *Away with you, Satan! For it is written, you shall worship the Lord your God, and Him only you shall serve"* (Matthew: 4:4–10).

There appears to be multiple names for Satan. A few of these names include Lucifer, Beelzebub, Belial, Mastema, the Prince of Darkness, and the lord of Lies. In the Bible, he was considered the accuser, the evil one, and the prince of the world. The ancient Hebrew language had a noun for Satan meaning obstructer or accuser.

> When the Old Testament was translated into Greek beginning in the third century B.C., Satan was rendered Diabolus, "adversary." From which come the Latin Diabolus, French Diable, German Teveel, English "Devil." The first time the word appears with a capital S, defining a particular person, is in the Book of Job. (Smithsonian, 1999, p. 1)

Satanism appears to have a tremendous and negative effect on adolescent criminal behavior. Engagement toward Satanism appears to be involved in crimes committed by teenagers. There appears to be a number of high profile cases in the 1980s that seem to document a connection between adolescent Satanism and violence. There are some teenagers who place the blame on Satan for their criminal careers. There was an Oklahoma teen that admitted to having killed his parents and a convenience store clerk because Satan instructed him to do so. Satanists sometimes engage in activities that are not only bizarre by conventional standards but also criminally oriented. Youthful Satanists should be classified as members of the satanic underground. Lowney (1995) found that "reputed participation in antisocial or criminal behavior activities of these individuals or groups are less structured and lack the organizational dimensions of the Satanic establishment" (p .2).

There is some research that supports that there is a correlation between Satanism and rebellion. Satanism has been portrayed by some as the ultimate rebellion; involvement in Satanism can be seen as an attractive activity to most rebellious youths.

Now that Satanism has been defined and clarified, let's now discuss a few other elements from Satan's kingdom. Witchcraft (Wicca) is one of the fastest growing elements of Satanism in today's society. The word "Wicca" means to send nature to one's service. According to research, demographics of Wiccans in the United States are challenging to find. The Wicca representative is very secretive and groups do not release membership roles. Current studies estimate that there are 3 million to 5 million Wiccans, and these numbers are increasing daily. Estimates cited by Berger and Christian-Apologist Craig Hawkins put the U.W. witch population at the mark of 150,000 to 200,000.

Edwards (1999) found "in a web survey conducted, 60 percent of respondents were under 30 and 62 percent were female. Berger found in her survey that 90 percent of respondents were white and well-educated" (p. 3).

Many adolescents find Wicca to be a sense of power. There appears to be a great spiritual hunger among adolescents in our society. This could be the initial draw of Wicca for girls. For a young teenage girl with no spiritual roots, Wicca offers and promises them power, which may lead one to be tempted. It would be appropriate to state that many individuals enter Wicca because they are reluctant to comply with domestic rules and regulations. Adolescents desire to make their own rules and do what feels good naturally as opposed to spiritually cleaving to the right thing! Wicca allows them to create their own religion, suitable to their own needs. In addition, many Wiccans are making efforts to increase their numbers through the Internet.

It is essential to state that teenage rebellion and disobedience did not occur overnight, but was very prevalent throughout the Old Testament. For example, let's review the biblical story of Jonah. God gave instructions to Jonah to go to Nineveh and preach the gospel. *"Arise, go to Nineveh, that great city, and cry against it; for their wickedness has come up before Me" (Jonah 1:2).* Jonah was reluctant to obey the authority of the Lord and went to Tarshish instead. Jonah's decision led him to experience severe consequences, which also jeopardized others who didn't fear God. It wasn't until Jonah went into the belly of the fish that he remembered the Lord.

> *When my soul fainted within me, I remembered the Lord; and my prayer went up to You, into your Holy Temple. But I will sacrifice to You with the voice of thanksgiving; I will pay that I have vowed. Salvation is of the Lord. So the Lord spoke to the fish, and it vomited out Jonah onto the dry land. (Jonah 2:7–10)*

If adolescents (juveniles) were obedient to authority, they would experience fewer negative consequences. The Bible states that youths should submit to the elder. "Likewise you younger people, submit yourselves to your elders. Yes, all of you be submissive to one another, and be clothed with humility: for God resists the proud, but gives grace to the humble" *(1 Peter 5:5)*. Authority is the response system by which all government, whether good or evil, is maintained. It is known that basic doctrine teaches us our relationship to God. However, spiritual authority teaches our relationships and responsibilities to each other!

One must acknowledge that witchcraft is a spirit that is very prevalent throughout the Bible. In the Old Testament, Saul went to a witch to inquire about his enemy David, even after he put away all those that had familiar spirits, and the wizards, out of the land.

> *So Saul disguised himself, putting on other clothes, and at night he and two men went to the woman. "Consult a spirit for me." He said," and bring up for me the one I name." (1 Samuel 28:8)*

40

It was Saul's intention to find out the status of his enemy David. The New Testament also makes reference to witchcraft. Witchcraft is known as the works of the flesh.

> *Idolatry, sorcery, hatred, contentions, jealousies, outbursts of wrath, selfish ambitions, dissensions, heresies, envy, murders, drunkenness, revelries, and the like: of which I tell you beforehand, just as I also told you in time past, that those who practice such things shall not inherit the kingdom of God. (Galatians 5:20–21)*

The practice of witchcraft and divination was a means for extracting information or guidance from a pagan god. Youngblood (1965) found that "the word describes the activity of Balaam the soothsayer (form of divination), or a professional prophet who was hired to curse Israel. It also described the woman at Endor who brought up the spirit of Samuel" (p.788). Sorcery was apparently practiced by the worst of the kings of Israel and Judah, but it was denounced by the prophets. *"And it came to pass, when Joram saw Jehu, that he said, is it peace, Jehu? And he answered, what peace, so long as the whoredoms of your mother Jezebel and her witchcrafts are so many? And Joram turned his hands and fled, and said to Ahazzah, there is treachery, of Ahaziah" (2 Kings 9:22–23).* According to biblical scripture, Nahum denounced the spirit of witchcraft.

> *Because of the multitude of the harlotries of the well seductive harlot, the mistress of sorceries, who sells nations through her harlotries, and families through her sorceries. Behold, I am against you, says the Lord of hosts; I will lift your skirts over your face, I will show the nations your nakedness, and the kingdoms your shame. I will cast abominable filth upon you, make you vile, and make you a spectacle. (Nahum 3:4–6)*

Conjuring spells is another practice that has witchcraft orientation. This phrase is known as "charm." Conjuring spells is also referred to as enchantments. A different Hebrew word lies behind this translation in *Isaiah 19:3*. Because it is related to a word for "bind," it may obtain the meaning of "casting a spell."

The book of *Isaiah* gives information pertaining to the Egyptians seeking charmers and other familiar spirits.

> *The spirit of Egypt will fall in its midst; I will destroy their counsel, and they will consult the idols and the charmers, the mediums and the sorcerers. (Isaiah 19:3)*

The majority of the research presented regarding witchcraft was based on both the Old and New Testament. One might pose the question, what about witchcraft today? Research indicates that many individuals fear witchcraft just as much as their ancestors did during earlier years. The primitive belief in hostile spirits is a universal experience of humanity. And despite what science and psychology have done to manifest the unknown and make the existence of evil spirits seems impossible, there are still people who suffer the feeling of something strange and uncomfortable present into their daily life. In many cases, this fear increases by the diabolic influence of sensational newspaper stories, inappropriate movies, and television shows. These picture strange characters practicing weird and often bloody rites.

One must not be oblivious to the fact that modern magic has a tremendous effect in our society. "Magic making" still survives in high-tech cities as much as its presentation in villages today.

> It thrives in the rites and ceremonies of a startling assortment of contemporary mystical groups, such as the druids, and the "craft" of modern witches, who call themselves "WICCA" (old English for "wise") to escape the association in so many minds of witchcraft with evil. (Hill, 1997, p. 58)

The Bible clearly states that we are constantly in a spiritual warfare. *(Ephesians 6:12)* God wants us to take on the whole armor of God, and the whole armor (Word) includes all ethnic groups, cultures, genders, and most pertinently, it includes juvenile delinquents. God wants us to have faith and believe in him. *"But without faith it is impossible to please Him: for he that comes to God must believe that He is, and that He is a rewarder to those who diligently seek Him"* (Hebrews 11: 6). Juveniles should first yield to the Spirit of God and allow God to cleanse them from all their unrighteousness. This will allow the Holy Spirit to lead them and guide them in their daily walk with Christ! To be more specific, juveniles must truthfully acknowledge the sin in their lives and then confess their sins to God. *"If we say that we have no sin, we deceive ourselves, and the truth is not in us. If we confess our sins, He is faithful and just to forgive us our sins, and to cleanse us from all unrighteousness" (1 John 1:8–10).*

It is God's intention to set individuals free from spiritual bondage. God calls us into liberty with love as the objective. Juveniles should redirect their experiences of darkness to an internal and external life experience of light. *"that you may proclaim the praises of Him who called you out of darkness into His marvelous light" (1 Peter 2:9).* Once a delinquent decides to turn his life over to Jesus Christ, one can allow the Holy Spirit to fight this spiritual warfare against the adversary, "Satan." When one accepts the Lord as their Lord and Savior, God will not allow them to be destroyed by the works of the dark forces. In addition, salvation brings an individual to a level of confidence in Jesus Christ!

> *The Lord is my light and my salvation: whom shall I fear? The Lord is the strength of my life; of whom shall I be afraid? When the wicked came against me to eat up my flesh, my enemies and foes, they stumbled and fell. (Psalm 27:1–3)*

One should remember that this spiritual warfare must be confronted through prayer and fasting. For example, a certain man came to Jesus who advocated for his son, who was a lunatic and "sore vexed." This certain man mentioned that he had brought his son to the disciples and they had been unable to heal him. In conclusion, Jesus was able to cast the demon out of the man's son. The disciples later questioned Jesus on why they couldn't successfully cast out the demon. *(Matthew 17:20-21)*

God has power over all the power of wicked spirits, witchcraft, and hexes. Through the power of prayer, these strongholds can be destroyed in the name of Jesus Christ. *"For the weapons of our warfare are not carnal but mighty in God for pulling down strongholds" (2 Corinthians 10:4).* Christians should understand that prayer is communication with God and that all individuals can offer prayer, but individuals who have not trusted Jesus Christ for their salvation continue to remain alienated from God. So, while unbelievers may pray, sinners do not have the basis for a rewarding fellowship with God. They have not met the conditions laid down in the Bible for effectiveness in prayer. It would be necessary to state that prayer changes things. Without the promise of prayer, things become useless. One's life becomes dim, voiceless, vacant, impersonal, and centers one in complete isolation. It is important to state that one must have a pure heart to receive a response from the Lord, especially when it concerns inheriting the Kingdom of God. *"Who may ascend into the hill of the Lord? Or who may stand in his holy place? He who has clean hands, and a pure heart. Who has not lifted up his soul to idol, nor sworn deceitfully" (Psalm 24:4).*

The commonality that juvenile delinquents and workers of witchcraft share is that their hearts have become too hardened to receive the Word of God. God can take away a stony heart and replace it with a heart of flesh. For example, God instructed Ezekiel to prophesy to the Israelites, who had profaned among the heathen. It was God's promise to bring the Israelites into their own land. *(Ezekiel 36:25–28)*

God acknowledges the heart of man. Iniquity can't be hidden from God at all. He searches the heart of humanity, as well as the mind. *"Now he who searches what the mind of the spirit is, because He makes intercession for the saints according to the will of God" (Roman 8:27).* Although one may sin in their life, God's love and grace overcomes any transgression! The delinquent, the witchcraft worker, or the murderer can be released from their sin and rest from their unhealthy labors. *(Matthew 11:28-30)*

God wants us to inherit rest from what the world offers. The Lord desires to call the chief sinner of the world into rest. He doesn't discriminate against anyone. Here is what Apostle Paul said: *"This is a faithful saying, and worthy of all acceptation, that Christ Jesus came into the world to save sinners: of whom I am chief" (1 Timothy 1:15).* Apostle Paul was able to classify himself as a chief sinner. Meaning that he was considered the head in leadership terms. Apostle Paul actually persecuted the church prior to his conversion and caused many Christians to be put to death. It is because of God's grace and love, he was saved from eternal damnation! All humans are able to experience the unconditional love of the Lord. God loves humanity in spite of their many transgressions and disobedience.

In this chapter, one can clearly see that there is a correlation between Satanism and the juvenile delinquent. Juveniles should come to a position where they are able to see that they are also victims of Satan as they perform labor for him by offending innocent individuals. Nevertheless, there is an omnipotent God who gives us power to overcome all fear. *"For God did not given us the spirit of fear; but of power and of love, and of a sound mind"* (II Timothy 1:7). I strongly believe that this is one of the many Christian prescriptions to victory!

It is evident that evil is present in this world. Although this evil exists, the Lord still wants to change to create a new person through us. *"Therefore, if any man be in Christ, he is a new creature: old things are passed away: behold, all things are become new"* (2 Corinthians 5:17).

If juvenile delinquents will yield to Christianity, God will destroy the evil in their lives and its operations. It is God's plan to put an end to Satan's works. *"The devil, who deceived them, was cast into the lake of fire and brimstone where the beast and the false prophet are. And they will be tormented day and night forever and ever"* (Revelation 20:10).

CHAPTER 6
THE CHURCH AND THE JUVENILE DELINQUENT

Quite often in our churches and communities, children experience a change in their development. However, children play a very prominent role in life. Jesus clearly mentioned his love and passion for children. For example, let us review *Mark chapter 9*. *"Whoever receives one of these little children in My name receives Me; and whoever receives Me, receives not Me but Him who sent me" (Mark 9:37–38).*

There are many scripture verses in the Bible that show a relationship between children and the Kingdom of God. *"Assuredly, I say to you, unless you are converted and become as little children, you will by no means enter the kingdom of heaven. Therefore whoever humbles himself as this little child is the greatest in the kingdom of heaven (Matthew 18:3–4).* In the gospel of *Luke*, Jesus also places significant emphasis on children.

It is evident that the Lord highlights children in the scriptures as a pattern, as well as an example on how Christians should model their life. Unfortunately, there are some children or adolescents who have never experienced a moment of high esteem or who have come from dysfunctional families. To be more specific, these individuals are often known in society as juvenile delinquents.

The goal of this chapter is to discuss the relationship between the church and the juvenile delinquent. Dysfunctional families often deprive adolescents of parental support, which can create a lack of positive role models, especially for African-American adolescents. The black church has a sense of foundation in the community.

> The black church is one of the primary institutional foundations of the black community. The black church family project surveyed a total of 635 northern churches, 320 in the north central and 315 in the northeastern US. Regarding the existence of youth support programs, one hundred and seventy-six churches reported having at least one program directed at adolescent non-members of the church, most of whom are from low-income homes. (Caldwell, 1994, p. 2)

Statistics show that older and more established churches were more likely to conduct youth programs than were the newer ones. For example, "among the newest churches (those less than 41 years old), only 23% reported youth programs. Among those 41–75 years old, the proportion rises to 32%. While among churches 76 years and older, 36% reported such participation" (Caldwell, 1994, p. 4).

In recent years, program implementers have increased attention on comprehensive prevention strategies that target family factors in reducing the onset and frequency of adolescent substance use. Community prevention programs will be discussed more as this book proceeds. There are many professionals who advocate that churches play a critical role in terminating social problems that are pertinent to juvenile delinquency. Churches and people of faith have a critical role to play in alleviating social issues, especially when it pertains to correcting juvenile delinquency and youth violence. The worker that addresses this problem with God will be more successful in working with juvenile delinquents.

It is also critical for individuals who work with juveniles to acknowledge the family dynamics that juveniles experience in their early developmental years. These children have experienced a void in their life. In many situations, the void for love is substituted by other early engagements. The provision of unconditional love with children counters the effects of harsh treatment they may have received in the past. Individuals who work with juveniles should not only acknowledge God but also demonstrate God through love in order to be successful. God gives us unconditional love, which was established when He sent

His son to die on the cross. Christians must comprehend why the Lord set His love upon us!

God's servants should also interpret the meaning of love. There are two different Greek words of love presented in the Bible. The word Phileo means to have ardent affection and feeling—which is a type of impulsive love. The other word, Agape, means to have esteem or high regard. For example, Jesus asked Peter if he loved him three times, and Peter responded positive from the questions of Jesus. Peter's love for Jesus was considered a Phileo version of love.

> So when they had eaten breakfast, Jesus said to Simon Peter, "Simon, son of Jonah, do you love Me more than these?" He said to Him, "Yes, Lord; You know that I love You." He said to him, "Feed My Lambs." (John (21:15–17)

In following the responses of Peter, one can determine that there were two types of love being displayed in the above passage of Jesus and Peter. Jesus expects us to demonstrate the type of love that He has given us. God wants us to model the kind of love that is both authentic and omnipotent. This kind of love is known as "Agape love." One can see that Jesus correlates love with feeding his sheep. Jesus persistently instructed Peter to feed His sheep if he proclaimed to really love Him. In the Old Testament, prior to David being anointed by Samuel, David was keeping the Lord's sheep.

> And Samuel said to Jesse, are all the young men here? Then he said, there remains yet the youngest, and there he is, keeping the sheep. And Samuel said to Jesse, send and bring him: for we will not sit down till he comes here. (1 Samuel 16:11)

According to the biblical story, David demonstrated his love for the Lord by feeding the Lord's sheep. David was in the presence of the Lord before he'd ever acknowledged his calling into the ministry. David was compliant to the Word of God, even as an adolescent. David acknowledged his purpose, as well as the objective of God's mission and purpose for His children.

The problem that juveniles face is that they don't have love *(John 3:16)*. Therefore, they are not displaying the character of God. The Bible declares, *"every spirit that does not confess that Jesus Christ has come in the flesh is not of God" (1 John 4:3)*.

It would be appropriate to state that when one is functioning at their true purpose, they are functionally at ease, fulfilled, and self-actualized. On the contrary, when we are unaware of our true purpose and calling, additional abuse occurs. In order to discover one's true purpose in life, several questions must be asked: Who am I? What was the reason of my creation? Who created me? What is my history? What is my future? To properly answer these fundamental life questions is to first understand one's purpose through Christ.

There are some Christians who believe that the church needs to resemble and model the Old Testament brother Nehemiah. Rev. Bruce Wall, author of *Setting At-Risk Free Through Spiritual Growth,* indicates the following about Nehemiah:

> He struggled to rebuild walls. I'm trying to rebuild
> the wall of protection around the youth I love and
> the youth I work with. We need a holistic approach
> to reaching young people. I think some churches
> make mistakes. I think some of us make mistakes
> in the church. We say we've got to get them saved.
> We count up how many we got saved and then we
> walk away from them. (Wall, 1995, p. 174)

It is important that children develop a form of connection with a Christian youth leader, or parent (guardian), who is involved in their lives. The connection must first be established between God and the individual working with the adolescent. The leader must first be right with the Lord before he/she can effectively connect anyone else to God. For example, one father who shared that he is no longer an active church member simply states, "I have a daily connection with God. It's not a Sunday thing. It's an everyday thing" (Bright, 1996, p. 252).

Church leaders have a tremendous responsibility within the congregation. The pastor should be aware of family dynamics. An important part of a pastor's ability to work effectively with both victims and survivors of abuse is from a theological orientation.

Beliefs regarding the family—the role of parents, children, and spouses and what is expected of each individual—can have powerful effects on the pastor's ability to respond with sufficient understanding and sensitivity.

The word pastor is known as "The feeder / protector, guide, or shepherd of a flock of God's people" in New Testament times. The term also implies to the nourishing of and caring for God's people. The prophet Jeremiah was instructed to help restore God's servants who were serving as a detriment to the Lord's children. *(Jeremiah 23:1-2)*

The calling of a pastor obtains a high level of responsibility because it entails feeding the Lord's children. The pastoral position is not the only leadership position that can optimistically affect the life of a juvenile delinquent. The book of Ephesians presents other Divine callings in the church area. *"And he Himself gave some to be apostles, some prophets, some evangelists, and some pastors and teachers, for the equipping of the saints for the work of the ministry, for the edifying of the body of Christ" (Ephesians 4:11–12).* According to the above biblical text, it is evident that the Lord uses positions in unity for the purpose of edifying the church body. For example, the calling of an evangelist is to proclaim the gospel of Jesus Christ geographically. The evangelist is an individual that is authorized to proclaim the gospel of Jesus Christ (that sounds like Christians!). The evangelist was a gift of God to the early church. These persons were not attached to any particular local church. They traveled over a wide geographical area, preaching to those to whom the Holy Spirit led them. In addition, the early disciples were also called evangelists because they proclaimed the gospel.

The pastor is stationed in the church; therefore, he should be aware of the multiple issues that youth encounter on a daily basis. Pastors should be meticulous in their approach with youths. In many cases, youths find it necessary for their physical, spiritual, and mental survival to reject the religious organizations that prohibit them from doing fun things, to have feelings, or expressing their emotions in abnormal ways. Therefore, they feel they must escape from such a system.

Children must be taught to honor their mother and father. One of the most familiar of the Ten Commandments instructs one to honor one's mother and father. *"Honor your father and your mother, that your days may be long in the land which the Lord your God given you" (Ex. 20:12)*. The above commandment has an emphasis based on the assumption that every child has a unique relationship to his or her parents. This may be commonly conceived as a natural obligation, which is an obligation rooted in the act of birth. Young people must be brought back to the foundation of religion and depart from their self-religious beliefs. It appears that adolescents often seem to separate from the institutional religion they were part of as children. As children, they obediently attended the religious school and religious services with their parents. However, as adolescents, they become resistant to participating in church activities. I asked myself the question why. I strongly believe that adolescents are reluctant to attend church because they perceive it to be boring. I can recall attending church services as an adolescent that were so boring that I occasionally fell asleep during services. I can honestly tell you that youths like to be stimulated and challenged in a recreational, leisure, and entertaining setting. Adolescents need to know that it's okay to have fun and still remain a Christian. In the early adolescent stage, the young person does not necessarily become less religious, rather they put their faith in personal religion to the exclusion of institutional religion. The Bible gives Christians instructions to be cognizant of doctrines—or philosophies of man that are deceitful and not Christ-like. *"Beware lest anyone cheat you through philosophy and empty deceit, according to the tradition of men, according to the basic principles of the world, and not according to Christ" (Colossians 2:8)*.

Adolescents must be led away from these unrighteous doctrines and from the mentality of individualism. One must learn to be in self-denial. The scripture declares, *"if any man will come after me, let him deny himself, and take up his cross, and follow me" (Matthew 16:24)*.

The challenge with humanity is that human kind does not want to die. Yes, we talk about life after death and what heaven has to offer us. However, one has to first die to selfish desires that do not include the Holy Spirit. Unfortunately, it's hard for adults to do this and even harder for adolescents. *Matthew 16:24* is a very simple scripture verse. Although there may be some adolescents who comprehend this scripture verse, there are those who need authority figures (leaders) to teach them ethics and morals. In general, adolescents need adults to exercise unilateral authority when it pertains to values, manners, and morals. In addition, adolescents themselves need to exercise mutual authority in matters of personal style and taste. Adults should not dictate to young people the kind of clothes they should wear, the types of food they should eat, or even the kind of music they desire to listen to.

It is important for youth leaders to appreciate how necessary it is for them to exercise authority. The leader should state his/her own position clearly and decisively with respect to sexual activity, substance abuse, foul language, pornography, and other negative manufactures. It appears that youth leaders obtain a great level of accountability for their daily youth ministry endeavors. The leader must be biblically equipped to work within the ministry. The Bible clearly presents the significance of one studying the Word of God. Apostle Paul encourages Timothy to *"be diligent to present yourself approved to God, a worker who does not need to be ashamed, rightly dividing the word of truth" (2 Timothy 2:15).* The book of *Titus* also gives wisdom on how young leaders must present themselves in the ministry. *(Titus 2:6–8)*

Troubled youths should be converted to the Word of God for a change in society, and the change should be initiated within the Christian body.

God intended the Christian faith to be the foundation of our lives. Christianity isn't a religion in the sense of a collection of formal and traditional rituals to follow. It's a way a person lives their life—a moral code of ethics! It is quite obvious that the church has a great responsibility to teach children the way of the Lord and parents are obligated to help their children comprehend the core of the Bible. Teaching our children about God and passing the basics of the Christian faith on to them isn't and shouldn't be considered abnormal. Christians should try to help them understand our traditions and the particular way in which we express and celebrate our faith in Jesus Christ!

It is also necessary to state that parents are not perfect and that child rearing takes time and energy, but it's well worth the effort! The parents who have always had an adequate relationship with their child have a head start on good relations with their adolescent. It's important to realize that all is not lost for parents whose style tends to be permissive, dictatorial, or even neglectful. If one can learn to be a responsive parent, the adolescent's behavior will improve.

There were many statements that were discussed in this section pertaining to the parental responsibility with emphasis on adolescents. As briefly discussed earlier in this chapter, the church carries a prominent responsibility when it concerns the salvation of one's soul.

According to the book of *Matthew*, Jesus commissioned the church to make disciples and teach them what He had taught them. The book of *Acts* also advocated for pursuing the commission of Jesus Christ. In fact, the book of Acts is the story of the early church's struggle to be loyal to this commission. One can see the significance of the church and the impact it plays in the community environment. It would be appropriate to state that the church body must assist in rooting the at-risk youth in the Word of God; young people would then turn away from the offerings to a world that promotes no blessing. Youths need to become rooted in faith and rooted in a relationship with the Lord. If not, they will continue to become involved with drugs, teenage pregnancies, suicide, satanic worship, and other self-detrimental things.

Church leaders should be able to encourage young people so that they will desire to do better in their daily activities. It is also important that leaders become able to discern the specific areas in one's life that needs improvement and deliverance. Leaders should tell kids that they want them to improve and get better. If you're going to help people who are at risk, you've got to say to them: I know where you are in your life right now. I see how you're moving. Let's analyze how you're making this progress. It's realistically finding out how the youth can be better next time, as well as finding out how you can help the youth improve and perform to their abilities.

Peer counseling is another effective method that can be utilized in the church. Children can both counsel and peer-tutor each other. This is beneficial because they will reveal information to their peers that they would discuss with a professional. The Old Testament book of *Proverbs* gives reference of the significance of counsel. *"Where there is no counsel, the people fall; but in the multitude of counselors there is safety" (Proverbs 11:14).*

As a Christian leader, one should be able to direct an incoming delinquent youth to the right counselor, our Lord and Savior Jesus Christ *(Isaiah 9:6).*

The church should be an environment that has a loving, internal community. Bringing children up with the support of a loving, Christian community encourages and inspires others. In addition, parents are also supportive and helpful in the task of parenting. In many situations, juveniles do not have parents who demonstrate Christianity in their homes, as well as fathers in their lives. In situations like this, one must see the Lord as their ultimate father. *"When my father and my mother forsake me, then the Lord will take me up" (Psalm 27:10)*. It is the Lord's desire to lead the youth into his bosom and to feed and comfort them. The scripture states, *"He will feed His flock like a shepherd; He will gather the lambs with His arm, and carry them in His arm, and gently lead those who are with young" (Isaiah 40:11)*.

Adolescents are also battling with other challenges in their life. Among the most salient of the problems facing adolescents today are out-of-wedlock births. Adolescent pregnancy and out-of-wedlock births may have negative consequences such as poverty and a major delay in choice of employment and education. In regards to this, there is a need for the establishment of more youth programs within churches. These youth programs will not only present favorable alternatives for juvenile delinquents, but they should discourage poor social decisions (i.e. teen pregnancy and drug use). It is obvious that there are some churches that have youth programs for adolescents in need, but there is a need for an increase because of the multiple issues that adolescents are experiencing daily.

Christian counseling is one method that is also effective in working with the juvenile delinquent or adolescent at-risk.

CHAPTER 7
COUNSELING AND TREATMENT FOR JUVENILE DELINQUENTS

Adolescents are usually exposed to many people, places, and things within their environment. Although every experience is a learning one, juvenile delinquents encounter situations that may cause great disturbance in their lives. There are certain adolescents who overcome their negative experiences and convert into a more righteous seeking individual. Unfortunately, there are also those individuals who seem to sustain in the same negative efforts. Juvenile delinquency is a population that is notorious for being the most difficult and challenging group to work with. Delinquents experience difficulty in achieving an adequate adjustment to the demands of everyday life. For every delinquent that fails to conform to the rules and regulations of society, there is usually an explanation as to why his/her behavior exists.

The population of delinquents is steadily increasing and becoming more diverse throughout our society. The causes for acting-out, and the specific, related issues, may vary from urban to suburban to rural settings, but all communities consist of belligerent, nonverbal, and unmotivated adolescents and preadolescents. Juvenile delinquency does not appear overnight or even within the span of a year. There are usually premature notices that are expressed by the individual before they become a delinquent. Research shows that habitual and serious norm-violating behavior requires a fairly long period of time for its development. This means that many youngsters display hints or signs well before a pattern of norm-violating behavior is thoroughly established. It is disturbing to hear that there are juvenile delinquents who are lacking parental guidance and positive role models and therefore devote their energies to negative behaviors within the community.

Many juvenile delinquents are reluctant to benefit from the educational system and, in most cases, express misconduct in the learning atmosphere. Because a delinquent's parents (or guardians) are not usually present during school activities and functions, the classroom teacher fulfills the parental or authoritative role. The classroom teacher has a crucial and complex role to play in directly helping the children that constantly violate the norm. There are teachers who are professionally trained to work with youngsters and brought into close contact with them for extended periods of time. At least until they are referred to a more qualified professional who is trained to work with these youths.

When working with juvenile delinquents, it is important to establish a therapeutic approach, especially when it pertains to juvenile delinquents within group counseling. Many juvenile delinquents mature in environments where there is serious violence and crime. Delinquents may take advantage of any negative moment that's available because there is a great opportunity to engage in criminal activity. A delinquent's behavior is usually a cry in and out for help. There are many juveniles who have been hiding their tears for many years desiring help to come out of the windy storm. These tears eventually come out in an unhealthy manner.

There are some juveniles that not only lack adequate parental guidance, role modeling, and self-discipline, but may also be experiencing the various stages of adolescence. During this period, Erik Erickson believes that adolescents go through a period of crisis, whereby they experience a failure in achieving ego identity during their process of adolescent development.

I have reason to believe that between the ages of ten and eighteen is the stage at which we must meet and resolve the crisis of our basic ego identity. At this time, we form our self-image, uniqueness, self-perception, and ideas about ourselves and about what others think of us.

I believe that counseling with juvenile delinquents can be effective. Group counseling may enable one to ventilate feelings and emotions that may be a cause of previous and current behaviors. A juvenile delinquent will not only have the opportunity of expressing their self-awareness but they can share equivalent experiences in relation to other participants in the group and receive support from them as well. The most prevalent thing is the sharing of one's inner being and then the acceptance of others.

THERAPEUTIC APPROACHES

There are a variety of therapeutic approaches that can be utilized when counseling juvenile delinquents in a group setting. During my academic efforts, I have studied several theories and therapeutic approaches that are used with adolescents. I have found some of these approaches to be effective and others to be non-effective. Through observing multiple professional assessments and tools, I was able to formalize a therapeutic approach called **Christian Direct Intervention (CDI)**. This is no offense to other traditional therapeutic methods. I find that adolescents need a little more than just natural laws, hypnosis, and a prescription for Ritalin® that most continue to take into their thirties. ☺

I mention this because for centuries, psychologists, psychiatrists, and psychotherapists have made several contributions in trying to find a remedy for adolescents who demonstrate these types of negative behaviors. The benefit of **CDI** is that it provides direct intervention to the issues that are affecting the juvenile delinquent, as a whole. This is accomplished by targeting the three different areas consisting of spiritual, environmental, and natural relations. Among the many therapeutic approaches that can be used, **CDI** is a chosen therapy that can be used when working with juvenile delinquents, as well as children and adolescents who are displaying oppositional behavior. **CDI** makes certain assumptions about the spiritual, environmental, and natural existence of human beings and where one is positioned among these three elements. **CDI** is a therapeutic approach that can be used within an individual, family, and group therapy setting.

It is quite obvious that many juvenile delinquents have exhibit tendencies to think irrationally and allow their irrational thoughts to influence their behavior. I will first like to discuss the spiritual element of **CDI**.

Have you ever thought about what causes someone to do a particular thing? I often think of why a person would like to shoot another individual with a gun. Well, there are reasons why these actions occur.

The spiritual element plays a significant factor regarding human behaviors. We know that as Christians, we become born again by the Spirit of the Trinity (God) that consists of the Father, Son, and Holy Spirit, which equals one. Prior to a Christian's conversion, a person may have engaged in every unrighteous act under the sun! This is why Solomon stated, *"I have seen all the works that are done under the sun; and indeed all is vanity and grasping for the wind" (Ecclesiastes 1:14)*. Obviously, the worldly acts of a non-Christian are not pleasing in the eyes of God. The juvenile delinquent is not yet saved by the Spirit of the Lord and Savior Jesus Christ. Therefore, Satan is governing his/her activities. I have worked with several adolescents and adults who have mentioned experiencing auditory hallucinations and hearing spirits instructing them to kill someone or even having rapid homicidal ideations. These spirits are not of God. God will not place the order of death on anyone's life. His intention is for us to have abundant life. In the spiritual element, the juvenile delinquent must be subject to the Spirit of God in order for a spiritual intervention to occur.

The therapist or counselor should be able to spiritually access the individual in order to see the spiritual development of that client (juvenile delinquent). Once this is determined and the client submits to God's authority, then counseling can be accomplished. As with most therapy, a rapport must be established with the client prior to setting therapeutic goals.

The environment plays another important element in this therapy model. I strongly believe that people are a product of their environment. I am not saying that heredity school has no contribution to the personality or character of an individual. On the contrary, I believe that the environment has a greater impact. The question to ask is this: what is the product? The juvenile delinquent can develop his/her tendencies through observation of the home, school, neighborhood, and other environments. Here is a scenario that can be used to help describe the environmental element.

Ken is a fourteen-year-old male who enjoys staying after school with his friends to play baseball. Ken's friends are always sniffing cocaine behind the school's baseball field before playing baseball. Ken is the only individual among his friends who is not interested in drugs. One-day, Ken decided to give sniffing cocaine a try because he was tired of being teased about being a sissy and a mamma's boy. Ken became addicted to cocaine after a few experimental sniffs and has been to several substance abuse programs for the past four years.

One can conclude that Ken was influenced by his environment, and as a result, he began to engage in the same behaviors as his friends. This is only one example among many that can be used to describe the environmental element.

In order for an intervention to occur in this area, the professional must be direct in confronting the client's environmental choices and encouraging them to choose more healthy alternatives. This task is not as easy as it sounds. One can be successful once they establish an adequate rapport with the client.

The natural element is the final relation that has an effect on the juvenile delinquent. Have you ever heard of the saying, "let nature take its course?" This saying may be applied to certain situations, but when it pertains to juvenile delinquents it's just not good enough! If we allow nature to take its course with juvenile delinquents, it will ultimately be a natural disaster. I am not saying that nature is bad. God did not create anything bad. Bad turned bad all by its bad self! I'm simply talking about the natural existence of tangible things. Humans need food, clothes, and shelter among other natural resources. Some juvenile delinquents will engage in criminal activity in order to acquire these things. It may not be just food or clothes; it may be stealing a car, robbing someone at the subway station, or selling drugs for money. These natural reasons or acts are for natural motivations.

The professional working with the delinquent will assess and document the immediate needs of the client and help them develop methods in achieving these natural needs. As a therapist, I find that there are several resources in the community that can accommodate the needs of one who lacks certain essentials. These listings usually include shelter, food services, diverse counseling programs, mentors, etc. The professional must help the client exhaust all of these community resources. This may help reduce some of the behavioral patterns of the delinquent.

CDI can enable juvenile delinquents to look at their illogical behavior and the underlying causes of their actions through direct intervention. Although many variables can contribute to delinquent behavior, such as abandonment and negligence of the adolescent, it is important for juvenile delinquents to accept some responsibility for their negative acts. The delinquent's negative and self-defeating thoughts and emotions must be challenged by healthy perceptions in order for one to establish a rational and logical mentality. Juvenile delinquents can accomplish this through the usage of **Christian Direct Intervention** within an individual, group, and family therapy setting.

CDI Group Sessions can be held with juvenile delinquents once a week for a period of one year. Subjects will be screened and interviewed before entrance for the benefit of all individuals of the group. For example, if the majority of individuals have similar backgrounds—as they relate to spiritual status, environmental, and natural experiences—then the delinquent will be qualified to enter the group. In addition, an interview will be conducted with the parent (or guardian) and adolescent to assist them in creating goals for the benefit of the delinquent and family. The group will consist of ten to twelve juvenile delinquents, and one will perform as the facilitator to assure favorable progress of the group.

When counseling juvenile delinquents in a group setting, it is important to have a leader who is qualified to mediate the direction of the group participants. In most cases, the group leader is known as the facilitator. Group facilitation is aimed at enhancing the group experience and enabling the group members to reach their individual goals. Facilitation skills involve opening up clear and direct communication among the participants and helping them assume increasing responsibility for the direction of the group. In **CDI,** there are a variety of methods that the facilitator can use within the group process. Among the many methods, the following can be used when working with juvenile delinquents:

- Observing for resistance within the group and helping clients realize when they are holding back and the reasons why?

- Advocating for clients to openly disclose their feelings and expectations
- Encouraging and teaching members to talk directly, plainly, and respectfully to one another within the group setting
- Creating a comfortable environment and atmosphere of safety that will encourage clients to take risks during group sessions
- Offering a support system for clients as they experience new barriers
- Developing a client-to-leader rapport
- Allowing a healthy and open release of conflict
- Helping clients overcome barriers to direct communication
- Helping clients integrate what they are learning in the group and find ways for them to apply it to their daily lives
- Helping members achieve closure by approaching unfinished business in the group
- Monitoring client progress in the group sessions and presenting feedback to clients when necessary

GOAL OF THERAPY

When working with juvenile delinquents in a group setting, one should establish goals for the benefit of the individuals in the group. The objective of the goal is to enable individuals to reach a more positive level of success. These goals will encourage juvenile delinquents to focus on the present and future and avoid perpetuation of past negative experience. We should remember that the goal of therapy is to eliminate or reduce the irrational thoughts and behaviors, as well as emotional disturbances experienced by clients. Below are a few goals that are created for the participants of the group:

- Learn how to accept responsibility for one's actions
- Develop healthy and organized thought patterns
- Improve the communication system within the family unit and with other authoritative persons
- Develop positive choices and process of decision making

- Express unpleasant feelings and emotions; acquire empathy and support from group participants

If individuals of the group allow themselves to experience the above goals, they will not only change the manner in which they perceive internally and externally but they can also become self-aware of their verbalizations and actions, which may affect them or people in their environment.

TECHNIQUES OF THERAPY

While in the process of working with juvenile delinquents in the group session, there are many techniques that can be used with **CDI.** The techniques that are used in this group consist of **prayer, spiritual assessment, biblical readings, meditation clearance, Christian positive cognition, Christ-directive teaching, and complimentary buffet.**

Prayer is one technique that is highly needed in order for **CDI** to benefit the client. As a minister, I have learned that prayer is not only one of the elite foremost acts of Christianity, it is a prerequisite to change. The Christian professional may have to explain the benefits of prayer to the client(s). I have witnessed God move mountains in the life of families, loved ones, and thousands of people I have ministered to throughout ministry. If you think about it, God speaks to us through His Word, and we must speak to Him through prayer. Prayer is the only method of communication where information can be communicated to God from humanity.

Spiritual Assessment is important to do with the client prior to creating a treatment plan. During this assessment, the Christian therapist will spiritually examine the client in order to see where he/she is in their walk with God. **This is not a judgment call!** It is not appropriate to assume that a juvenile delinquent is distant in their relationship with the Lord because of ones behavioral patterns. The therapist should be able to confirm the client's status. Many juveniles are actually raised in the church, but they may have later made a choice to leave the church for a particular reason. On the contrary, there may be a client who has had no biblical training from their parents or ever experienced an intimate relationship with the Lord.

Biblical Readings may be voluntarily encouraged during the beginning of each session with individuals of the group. If the client is inclined to engage in readings from the Bible, I will recommend specific scriptures or prayers for the client's advantage. Biblical readings will allow the client(s) an opportunity to learn about Jesus and how He is able to solve one's arising issues through power and demonstration of the Holy Spirit. This technique will also help one establish a relationship with God and develop knowledge and understanding of His Word. Through both prayer and biblical readings, the client(s) may decide to receive Jesus Christ as their personal Savior and Lord.

The main objective of **Meditation Clearance** is to have the client(s) relax and meditate on the hostile experiences that may have played a role in their present conditions. When the client(s) has located these experiences, they will be asked to verbally and emotionally express their feelings. Once the participants have completed this procedure, they will be asked to clear their mind of any displeasing thoughts and feelings and replace it with positive views.

Persistent usage of this technique may help individuals develop a peaceful mentality. Obviously, the success of this technique is a gradual process, and clients must work at their own pace. If forced, clients can regress and their behaviors and thought patterns can become more detrimental to themselves as well as to others.

Christian Positive Cognition consists of pleasant statements and words that may be distributed to the client(s) for usage during periods of distress. It is my belief that if an individual listens and reads positive information, that individual will eventually adapt and follow in those same characteristics. It's easy to tell someone when he or she has done something wrong or is being improper. Positive recognition can serve as a pacifier to the one who is internally crying.

Christ-directive Teaching will be applied in working with juvenile delinquents. This technique will be used to reeducate the client(s) in order to develop a more righteous seeking and logical mentality. The client or participants will be shown that their interior sentences are illogical and unrealistic. The counselor will inform them that Jesus can help them in becoming a better person. After the initial stage, the professional assumes an active teaching role to reeducate the client. The professional demonstrates the illogical origin of the client's disturbance and the persistence of illogical self-verbalization that serve to continue the disturbance. In addition, present to them illuminating biblical methods that Jesus instructed and desires His followers to conform to.

The **Complimentary Buffet** is a very unique therapeutic technique that can be used with an individual, group, and family setting. In this form of therapy, the initiator (counselor, mature Christian) is given an opportunity to initiate discussion during a time of family gathering for meals. The initiator will voluntary release positive statements to every individual, group, or family member who is present at the table, and everyone seated at the table will be given an opportunity to verbalize "positive statements" to each other. The objective of this technique is to bring out the positives in the individual(s).

Think about it. It is so easy to find negative things to say to someone because of human's imperfections. If you spend your time looking for dirt then eventually you will find it if it exist! If you think about it, the earth is full of dirt! In actuality, all four corners of this earth consist of dirt and multiple colors of dirt. Juvenile delinquents are constantly hearing about something they did wrong or their inappropriate behaviors. If the professional utilizes this technique, the client(s) will have an opportunity to hear positive feedback, which will help improve the client's attitude and possible approach on life.

It's important to know that these techniques can ultimately help redirect the client(s) to the pathways of righteousness through the Holy Spirit's guidance and direction.

COUNSELING TERMINATION & FOLLOW UP

Counseling termination is usually the most difficult time that clients will have to experience. Prior to this stage, clients should have established an adequate clinical relationship with other participants. Therefore, the termination of the group is quite equivalent to the termination of the established relationship. The clients become aware that their counseling relationship is about to dissolve, and they are beginning to mourn their impending separation. Some of them may pull back, become less intense, and may no longer contribute or disclose information about themselves. It is even possible that the client(s) may express anger and transference towards the counselor.

After a period of one year in working with these juvenile delinquents within a group setting, the group may be terminated. The criteria for termination will consist of expression of feelings by the delinquent and an interview with their parent (guardian).

Within the structure of the group, it is necessary that members of the group be asked to disclose their current feelings pertaining to other participants and to the actual termination of the group. Expression of feelings will enable individuals to release any possible issues that were not expressed from previous sessions, as well as their feelings about the termination of the group.

The **Individual Centered Approach** will be used with the delinquents upon completion of therapy. The Individual Centered Approach places emphasis on active listening and exploring the client's feelings pertaining to his/her previous and present therapeutic issues. The therapist or counselor is able to center in on the different variables that are affecting the client's mental being. You would be surprised by the number of clients I've talked with who desired to kill themselves, and all they really wanted was someone to talk with who would listen to many of their trials and tribulations. I can recall phone counseling one client who indicated to me that he was feeling suicidal and had a loaded gun in his hand. The Lord led me to create a comfortable environment in order for the client to be able to disclose the traumatic emotions that had placed him in that suicidal state of mind. I realized that the individual was battling with many issues regarding unemployment, homosexuality, low self-esteem, insecurity, major depression, as well as other unspecified issues. After he expressed all of his hurt and pain, I then told him that he was special in the eyes of God and that God loves him unconditionally. The great thing that occurred was that he received God's Words and decided to not kill himself; instead, he requested mental health treatment. I was able to refer him to immediate services that would help him with his presented problems.

The professional must remember the importance of listening until the client allows you to speak. Yes, this is a very hard thing to do. I must be honest with you because I struggle with this myself. However, in order to be helpful to the client, you should first understand what the problem is before the solution can be offered. Here's an example.

My wife Keisha and I owned a vehicle that was very dysfunctional a few years ago. We spent hundreds of dollars trying to fix this vehicle and have used several local mechanics. One day, we finally decided to take our vehicle to the dealership for a more accurate diagnosis. The dealer diagnosed the vehicle and was able to determine exactly what area of the vehicle was defective. The vehicle was fixed.

The professional counselor must be able to assess what the problem is before utilizing their tools. If you think about it, how can a mechanic fix a car when he/she does not know what area of the vehicle is damaged? Christian professionals should also remember that Jesus Christ is our maker. Therefore, we ought to lead the client(s) to Jesus Christ by all righteous means necessary!

In regards to counseling youths, an interview with the parent (or guardian) is also an important factor regarding the termination of counseling. This will allow the parent (or guardian) and adolescent an opportunity to review any possible progress that may have been established within the counseling session. In addition, there will be a post meeting in order to confirm the progress of the delinquent's behavior with family and within the community.

CHAPTER 8
CHRIST AND THE
DEPRESSED ADOLESCENT

Adolescents find themselves living in a culture where changes in community, church, and family have removed many social supports they may have found in the past. This loss of support, connectedness, or placement in society also increases the likelihood of adolescent depression. In this situation, the adolescent is vulnerable of losing emotional control. An adolescent is a person who has needs and is happiest when these needs are met. In addition, God is also a great necessity in the teenager's life. There are some counselors who believe that teenagers have eternal souls and should be connected to the Lord. Satan may prevent them from finding Christ later. Researchers believe that the adolescent stage is probably the time when a teen will be the most responsive to the voice of God. There are many depressed teenagers who develop an inferior self-esteem or self-image. A teenager's choice of a low self-esteem or image may make it difficult for him/her to manage the various stressful situations they experience. The way you view and feel about yourself is primarily what image you will portray.

For example, if Susan presents confidence whenever she competes in her swimming events, then she has a greater chance of winning her events. Also, if Jim perceives himself as a terrible basketball player and believes that he will never improve his skills, then his chances of becoming a successful basketball player are very slim to none.

I believe that confidence defines where you are and where you are going. David in the Old Testament demonstrated confidence when he fought against the great Goliath of Gath, the

Philistine. David acknowledged that Goliath was a giant. David did not look at his size; he looked at the opportunity for success. Listen to what David said to Goliath.

> *"You come to me with a sword, with a spear, and with a javelin. But I come to you in the name of the Lord of hosts, the God of the armies of Israel, whom you have defied." (1 Samuel 17:45)*

Juvenile delinquents are faced with Goliaths on a daily basis. The professional's job is to help the juvenile delinquent identify these Goliaths, as well as impart biblical knowledge and instruction on how these Goliaths can be removed from their life.

It appears that in primitive years, adolescents obtained an adequate identity within the community, family culture, and religious community. Unfortunately, in this period of time, the pattern no longer exists, and there are many variables that may be a contributing factor regarding this matter. In previous years, adolescents were given concise family, cultural, community, and religious identities, and God was the God of their fathers and the King of Kings and Lord of Lords! Researchers believe that because the divorce rate is increasing rapidly, teens are no longer offered an adequate family identity. The majority of these factors contributes to, or enhances, an adolescent's depressive status. It is known that the family and religious foundation of a young person has an important bearing on his understanding and actions. The teenager is perceived as the product of many forces. These forces usually include such things as the home, church, school, friends, and reading materials. The majority of a teenager's behavior is usually a direct reflection of these areas of influence. The depressed adolescent who is planning on pursuing God should enhance his/her spiritual faith. Both our feelings and our faith operate through the same personality package. The Lord works in our life through our personalities. The mechanisms of our personalities, which we use in faith, are the same instruments through which our feelings are being operated.

There is psychological evidence that there appears to be a variety of depression symptoms among adolescents. These symptoms include inadequate academic performance, substance abuse, anti-social behavior, sexual promiscuity, truancy, and in some cases, running away. A great benefit about accepting Jesus Christ into an individual's life is that one will never be alone. *"And I will pray the Father, and he will give you another helper, that He may abide with you forever; I will not leave you orphans: I will come to you"* *(John 14:16–18).*

Christian researchers learn that Jesus does not want his children to suffer the pains within society. Jesus acknowledges the infirmities among humans. Jesus Christ our high priest has already been touched with the feelings of our infirmities. Jesus, the Son of God, identified with us humans when he put on humanity. He not only knows our infirmities but also our feelings and emotions. Jesus understands the pain of rejection and affliction, the anxiety of separation and isolation, the terror of loneliness, neglect, and abandonment, and the gloomy clouds of depression.

Throughout my experience as a minister and therapist, I have witnessed Jesus save several adolescents from depression and the arena of the enemy. Mental and spiritual treatment play a significant role when concerning adolescents. There are additional treatment strategies and techniques that can be used for the benefit of bringing healing to depressed youths. This section deals with treating depressed adolescents with Jesus Christ.

There seems to be great discussion when it concerns the treatment process with depressed individuals. There have been studies suggesting that Christians often express a desire to have a therapist with similar religious beliefs. It is likely that established Christian approaches would be particularly helpful in providing services to Christians who will mainly seek services from Christian providers. The treatment strategies that will be expressed in this book are Christian-oriented. Although the treatment process is quite similar among adolescents and elders, it will be appropriate to separate these two populations because of minor approaches.

> Socrates once said that if he could get to the highest place in Athens he would lift up his voice and ask the citizens why they were turning every stone to scrape wealth together, yet taking so little care of their children to whom they must one day relinquish all. (Narramore, 1960, p. 133)

71

In order for the youth counselor to establish a rapport and a sympathetic kinship with a client, it is helpful for the counselor to understand the history of the adolescent. The teenager knows when an adult understands them; this acknowledgment helps facilitate the counseling process. One of the most significant contributions a Christian counselor can make to the life of an adolescent is to point out the power of the Holy Spirit who dwells within them. Since the adolescent years are conversion years, the Christian counselor should make every effort through individual counseling to lead youths to a saving knowledge and wisdom of Jesus Christ. The individual with a severe mental state of depression is seriously ill and needs skilled, professional diagnosis and treatment.

Depression in adolescents may develop itself in both behavioral and affective symptoms, which is different from what is observed in adult clients. For example: Aggression, hyperactivity, mood changes, and other forms of misbehavior may be as or more prevalent than the expected dysphoria often seen in adults. The development of a carefully pertinent diagnosis and intervention method relies on an accurate assessment of the client's mood, observable and consistency of behavior, as well as the familial environment.

There are many scales, checklists, or inventories that can be utilized during assessment with depressed adolescents. It is known that paper and pencil checklists regarding assessing depression are highly acceptable when working with adolescents. These checklists include the Child Depression Inventory, the Reynolds Adolescent Depression Scales, and the Children's Depression Scale. The measures are known to rely upon self-report from the client and are most useful when used in conjunction with other assessment methods. Researchers believe that the assessment of the client should include measures that allow for the evaluation of overall functioning. This includes intellectual and cognitive capacities, academic skills, as well as personality.

Christian Cognitive Behavior Therapy (CBT) is a model that is most effectively used with depressed adolescents. Lipsker & Oordt (1990) found that "CBT models of depression analyze the perceptions, beliefs, thinking, and evaluations of the client, as opposed to the performance of discrete, overt behaviors, as the key to developing an understanding of the problem" (p. 31).

Research presents five elements that are used in CBT. The elements of this approach are as follows:

Self-monitoring – Research shows that the use of self-report checklist and daily logs of activities, religious activities including prayer, church, youth group attendance, bible reading and study, as well as God related attributions which are reflected in cognitions are easily operationally defined and monitored.

Activity schedules – Working with the client in systematic planning of daily schedules, setting goals, and increasing participation in social activities. In addition, working with the family, teachers, and church workers may enhance the effort.

Cognitive reconstruction – This approach attempts to reframe, restructure, or realign cognitive patterns, which are seen as maladaptive.

Attribution retraining – Refers to the cognition activity of interpreting external events, particularly in regard to sources of control over events that occur in the adolescent's life.

Although Christian cognitive behavior therapy is recommended in the usage of counseling Christian adolescents, researchers optimistically believe that C-CBT model will become more thorough in the near future. Christian cognitive behavior therapy can be used with depressed individuals, but it is more prevalent among adolescents suffering from depression.

Jesus Christ surely does not want us to live our life alone. Human beings do not function well alone; to isolate oneself is to create a continuing mental deficiency. Biblical reading is considered to be one of the most effective methods utilized with depressed individuals seeking Christ. The bible states, *"teaching them to observe all things that I have commanded you; and, lo, I am with you always, even to the end of the age. Amen"* (Matthew 28:20).

Studies suggest that the relationship between prayer and depression is similar to the relationship between sunlight and darkness. The quantity of sunshine we allow to enter our houses is mainly the decision that everyone must make!

The pastor or Christian counselor is often in a position of

unique helpfulness to individuals in emotional distress and crisis. The professional can differentiate, in individual instances, between the transient reactions of normal personalities to stresses and strain and the profound disruptions of mental operation that are manifest in serious mental illness.

As indicated earlier, the assessment and evaluation process is quite essential prior to counseling the depressed adolescent. Studies show other inventories, questionnaires, and scales that can be offered during counseling. These include the automatic thoughts questionnaire (measures the frequency and occurrence of automatic negative cognitions); Rational Behavior Inventory (provides an overall measure of rationality); Beck Depression Inventory (constructed to measure clinical depression); as well as the religious behavior scale (assess frequency of several religious behaviors such as prayer, scripture reading, and church involvement).

There appears to be other forms of treatment that can be used with the depressed individual who is seeking Christ. Christian Rational-Emotive Therapy is one method that is highly recommended among Christian counselors. Christian Rational-Emotive Therapy is a version of Ellis' Rational Emotive-Therapy. The Christian version is known to have equivalent beneficial effects for depressed Christian clients. Although CRET is similar to RET in many ways, CRET uses the Bible rather than human reason as a guide to truth. Clients are encouraged to use vigor in their disputations and to work at enhancing their tolerance of discomfort and frustration.

All of these inventories and therapy approaches can be beneficial to the behaviorally challenged individual and adolescents who fall into the juvenile delinquency population.

COUNSELING IMPLICATIONS

It is important for Christian counselors (therapists) to understand the client and the various obstacles that may be before them. The depressed adolescent is most likely to pursue assistance from Christian leaders who present their interest in counseling. The counselor must be acute in observing the signals that the depressed person may be sending out. The counselor should devote their "elite" efforts during a session and "listen" to the one who needs to be "heard." In addition, the professional counselor should not become discouraged if a large portion of their cases fail. As a counselor, one is vulnerable to making mistakes and clients can become reluctant to change for the better. I believe that no one should be better qualified to counsel than the true man of God that understands the process of counseling. This individual has accurate insight into human nature and true wisdom and understanding. Through His Word, the believer finds the answers to life's problems, which the client(s) may be struggling with. The man (woman) of God should educate themselves with counseling course work.

Counselors and psychotherapists working with adolescents should be aware of the role that Christianity plays in the lives of individuals and the relation it has with mental health.

CHAPTER 9
THERE IS NO CONDEMNATION

I have great evidence to believe that the term "condemnation" has been birthed in the heart of the nation. Condemning has developed into a spirit unleashed in places of tranquility and saturated love. It has become an epidemic that has caused the death of both healthy and potentially healthy beings. **Why is it that people condemn each other? Who is the advocate of condemnation? How is condemning detrimental in working with the juvenile delinquent?** These are only a few questions that will be addressed in this chapter, but let us first define the word condemnation. Condemnation basically means to declare that an individual is guilty and has met the requirements of punishment in a judicial form. This means that the person being condemned must present their self to a judge or supreme judicial representative to be sentenced for a type of behavioral difference from the norm of society. This is a more technical definition of condemnation. A more superficial meaning is to magnify the negative thoughts or actions of a person in an effort to bring emotional and spiritual death to an individual. I can continue to give long definitions, but I think you have already grasped the concept!

The purpose of this chapter is to discuss the existence of condemnation and to explore the variables that exist regarding the sin of condemning and ultimately, how it can affect the rapport in working with juvenile delinquents. I think it's important to discover the reasons why people condemn each other as well as to highlight and discuss these possible reasons. Jesus stated in the scripture, *"Judge not, that you be not judged. For with what judgment you judge, you will be judged: and with what measure you use, it will be measured back to you"* (Matthew 7:1–2).

77

WHY IS IT THAT PEOPLE CONDEMN EACH OTHER?

As you probably already know, there are thousands of people who condemn on a daily basis. All of us have been guilty of this sin at one time or another. These individuals entail both the saved and unsaved population. As Christians, we know that the Word of God instructs us not to condemn anyone because it's just not the righteous thing to do! *"There is therefore now no condemnation to those who are in Christ Jesus; who do not walk according to the flesh, but according the Spirit" (Romans 8:1).* I have reason to believe that part of the reason why people condemn is because they have not yet fully acquired enough practical experience in not condemning. If people used more time in spiritual encouragement as opposed to condemnation, the world would be a much healthier place to live.

The problem that we face is that there are many people who are in bondage and have not yet been set free from their MASTER! This may imply that people should be set free from Jesus—as in move away from Jesus. Apostle Paul also made it clear in the book of *Galatians* that Christians should not be entangled with the yokes of bondage. *"Stand fast therefore in the liberty which Christ has made us free, and do not be entangled again with a yoke of bondage" (Galatians 5:1).*

People also condemn because they have been trained to do so. Children learn to condemn from their parents or guardians. There are many parents and school teachers who subconsciously make this error of condemnation. The child that acts out domestically or during class session is usually labeled as the "bad child." It's unfortunate that this child will travel with the same label throughout their academic experience at their school. Yes, it's essential to punish a child when they have violated domestic and public rules and regulations. However, don't sentence them to eternal death when the Lord has offered them eternal life. Jesus made it plain and clear that He did not come into the world to condemn anyone but for the purpose of offering salvation to the sinners of the world. The same condemning spirit that has been imparted to many parents is being placed on their children, and they eventually participate in the same sin. This generational curse should be broken before it prohibits more Christians and potential Christians from entering the Kingdom of God.

I once heard of a child who attended a prestigious local private school. This child had a tendency to misbehave in class and, at times, was non-compliant towards the rules of the classroom. One day, the teacher looked at the child and demanded that the child look into her eyes. She then stated, "You will never amount to anything." Fortunately, the child used this as a motivator throughout his life and became one of the most successful individuals in his generation. I suppose that the teacher believed that she was trying to motivate the child. Obviously, this method was not very beneficial at all. Although the child was not totally "in Christ Jesus," the teacher proclaimed to be. Therefore, her job was not to condemn the child but to correct the child in a loving manner.

I can't tell you how many people I know and have heard of who refuse to go to church because they were condemned by another Christian(s) in the church. Although this is a poor excuse for not attending church, one must be sensitive to the fact that these decisions exist. The Christian professional must remember that they themselves are not yet perfect, and they must be able to demonstrate patience instead of condemnation. I think it's important for Christian professionals to take inventory of themselves to see if they have unintentionally picked up a condemning spirit. There are many benefits of taking personal inventory. The Bible indicates, *"But let a man examine himself"* (1 Corinthians 11:28). The problem with this is that many individuals are quick to examine others prior to examining themselves.

I can recall looking in the mirror one morning while attending graduate school at the University of South Florida; then the Holy Spirit instructed me to look a little closer into the mirror. As I took a closer glance, I realized that I had several blemishes on my face that had dark tones. This is when the Lord reminded me that I was not perfect and from that day, I began to make changes in myself. I also began to view humanity in a different manner. It's important for us to remember that God is the only perfect and supernatural being. This is why Jesus is able to command us to not participate in condemnation. The problem with man is that man believes that they can be righteous without God. *"All the ways of a man are pure in his own eyes; but the Lord weighs the spirit's"* (Proverbs 16:2). In actuality, man can never be righteous. What's righteous is the Spirit of God that has been placed in humanity from a rebirth. Righteousness is the Lord who sent His son to an earth of multiple sin. Who died on the cross and was resurrected and ascended from an earth full of dead man's bones.

The Bible discussed how the scribes and Pharisees brought a woman to Jesus who had committed adultery. The scribes and Pharisees desired for the woman to be stoned to death under the law of Moses. It was wonderful how Jesus handled the situation. Jesus stooped down and wrote with His finger on the ground as if He did not hear the people, and His response was this: *"He who is without sin among you, let him throw a stone at her first"* *(John 8:7)*. The scripture later shows how the people felt convicted and walked away and left Jesus and the woman standing there. There was one powerful thing that Jesus said that pertains directly to this chapter. Let's listen a little further to God's wisdom.

> When Jesus had raised Himself up and saw no one but the woman, He said unto her, woman, where are those accusers of yours? Has no one condemned you? She said, no one, Lord. And Jesus said to her, Neither do I condemn you; go and sin no more. *(John 8:10–11)*

The lesson that we all can learn from Jesus is that He did not condemn the woman and He corrected the scribes and Pharisees from condemning as well. Jesus allowed the woman to go and instructed her not to sin in that act. Here, one can surely see God's unconditional love and saving grace.

The Christian needs to model the exact methods and techniques that Jesus engaged in. Yes, it means that we must be able to love even the one who has violated the commands of God. The scripture reminds us that *"all have come short from the glory of God."* Therefore, we are really not in the position to judge anyone at anytime.

WHO IS THE ADVOCATE OF CONDEMNATION?

I have learned that there is always a source or head of every organization, agency, establishment, event, and evil existence.

Therefore, there is someone who leads someone to condemn another person, and it does not just happen automatically. It is obvious that the adversary is the one that enables someone to condemn another person. Let's examine this a little further. The adversary (Satan) has a mission that entails stealing, killing, and destroying. You may be wondering what stealing, killing, and destroying has to do with condemnation, but I'm getting ready to tell you. If the adversary has stolen a person's joy, then he has been successful. If the adversary has killed someone's light of praising the Lord, then he has been successful. If the adversary has destroyed your intimate relationship with God and the church body, he has been successful in his mission. These are some things that occur during the act of condemnation that can be detrimental to the person who is being condemned.

The adversary's time on earth is extremely limited, so he is working overtime to discourage God's children in the best possible manner. His desire is to cause havoc in the church in order to bring division to relationships and the general church body. However, if detected early, he can be cast out of the church and out of the person that he is using. Satan is the cause for implanting these condemning spirits into the minds and hearts of God's children. I am not glorifying Satan, I am simply trying to warn you of his devices. I find it fascinating at times when I hear people who profess to be Christians express that they hate a particular person. Christianity is not based on hate, but love. Love must be the root and foundation of the Christian's interaction and participation in a world that rejects love. The only being that Christians should dislike and disown is Satan. There is no meeting place or median between light and darkness. If you think about it, light is designed for the purposes of vision or sight. Therefore, vision cannot be seen in the midst of darkness, but it brings light to darkness. In discussing the ministry of Jesus, the Bible states, *"the people who sat in darkness have seen great light, and upon those who sat in the region and shadow of death light has dawned"* (Matthew 4:16).

It is the adversary's desire to cause one to condemn another individual to bring emotional instability to the victim of condemnation, leading the victim away from the church through negative experiences. The individual will begin to associate the church with pain as opposed to a place of healing. One may begin to search for healing in the world and unexpectedly enter the adversary's territory. I can recall a church brother telling me a story about an evangelist who wanted to see what was so special about pornographic movies, so she decided to view one of these movies at a theater. In result, she picked up a demonic spirit. The following Sunday, when the evangelist went to church, she found her way at the altar after the pastor discerned something different about her during service. When the evangelist went to the altar, a demonic spirit said to the pastor, "She came into my territory."

Well, guess what? The adversary still has his same old tricks. Things remain the same with him because the time of the beast is short. Christians and counselors can create more damage to a client than good by condemning.

How Is Condemning Detrimental When Working With Juvenile's?

In this section of the chapter, I will discuss condemnation and relate it to the effect condemnation has on juvenile delinquents and how it can be detrimental to the delinquent client. The professional working with the delinquent must understand that the juvenile delinquent can be a very internally delicate individual. I know that this sounds very surprising due to the external character of a juvenile. The juvenile wants you to think that he/she is as hard as a rock and that nothing can disturb them or break them, but this is just a fabrication of who they really are. Deep down inside, the delinquent is a child crying out for help. This adolescent child has been crying out for help for quite some time, desperately seeking to be pacified. Unfortunately, the juvenile's pacifier comes from a world that pacifies one with violence, parental disobedience, hatred, lack of forgiveness, truancy, drugs, and many other negative contributors.

In working with juvenile delinquents, it's important for the professional to establish a rapport that is firm enough to hold a foundation. This foundation can also be known as a therapeutic relationship. In a therapeutic relationship, the client is able to trust the therapist and their treatment methods and strategies. Obviously, this does not occur overnight. Trust is a process and will eventually come into existence when the client has reason to believe that the therapist is available for their best interest and their interest only. You're probably wondering, what does condemnation have to do with this!

The juvenile delinquent has heard on several occasions how insignificant and detrimental he/she is in the community and that they will never amount to anything of purpose. Therefore, the delinquent should be comforted and not condemned, embraced and not rejected, loved and not hated!

The consequences of condemning a juvenile delinquent are very severe. The juvenile needs to know that they are someone special and not just a burden to society. I know that this may sound challenging to believe, but it's the truth. The more love and compassion that is shown to the juvenile, the greater the chance that one will be able to establish an adequate rapport with them.

I could never really understand the cause of war and exactly why the United States entered war on several occasions. Historically, the United States went to war with Iraq due to the offensive leadership of Saddam. The United States won the war and shortly after, President Bush declared the war finished. The unique thing about this is that the United States will spend billions of dollars rebuilding what they have already destroyed. If you think about this, it really does not make sense at all! Why destroy something that eventually will be rebuilt? The intention is not to say anything negative about the U.S. Government but to stimulate your mind a little and to prepare you for what I'm about to say. If we apply this to professionals working with juvenile delinquents, one can see that the juvenile delinquent is already at spiritual warfare and do not need any further affliction to their spiritual condition. The juvenile needs to be rebuilt into the vessel that God has intended for the adolescent before the foundation of the world. It does not matter what negative behaviors the adolescent has previously engaged in; he/she should be treated with love and given a chance to make a difference.

I can recall speaking to a group of juvenile delinquents at a high school in Tampa, Florida in 1995. During this presentation, a juvenile stated that he is likely to turn out to be a "thug" because his parents also made bad decisions during their life. I then realized that this particular adolescent would probably eventually fall into the same category as his parents by evidence of his mind set, unless a Divine Intervention occurred. This adolescent had already convinced himself that he was not going to accomplish anything with his life.

Our society places a lot of emphasis on developing the human mind. I strongly believe that society places a little too much focus on the mind, but that's another story for another book! Have you ever heard of the saying, "A mind is a terrible thing to waste?" One can conclude that the adolescent described above has told himself in his mind that he will not be successful, or ultimately, he will not walk in the blessings that God has ordained for him.

Satan likes to get in the mind of both the believer and unbeliever. If he can get into your mind, he can control your actions, and if he can control your actions, he will lead you to the pit of hell. The adversary's aim and determination is to steal the delinquent for his deceptive kingdom, kill God's will for the adolescent, and if this is too challenging for him, he wants to destroy the adolescent by any means necessary! As with most attacks of the adversary, this can only be accomplished if the adolescent allows himself to be deceived by Satan. If you are an adolescent and you are reading this book, I have a message for you. DON'T LET THE ADVERSARY ROB YOU OF YOUR LIFE, YOUR DREAMS, AND YOUR GOALS IN GOD'S WILL! I tell you this passionately because God loves you and wants the best for you. He wants you to live a life of happiness and fun in His Divine will. If you are a professional and you are reading this book, I also have a message for you. DON'T CONDEMN JUVENILE DELINQUENT'S—LOVE AND EMBRACE THEM! This is the only opportunity that the delinquent has, in most cases, to experience true love from a stable individual.

The professional counselor, therapist, or minister that works with juvenile delinquents should be totally committed to the task. In my secular work experiences, I have worked in jobs where I have witnessed employees working for the agency just to acquire a bi-monthly check. Yes, we know that money is required to take care of domestic responsibilities and other expenses of life; however, money should not be the motivating factor in working with disadvantaged youths or in any other social service area. I find that adolescents are able to discern if an employee is committed or just there for a paycheck. I have heard several youths voice this in my presence regarding staff agency members. I challenge the professional to put a dent in Satan's territory. Let the adversary acknowledge who is the real boss and that he is going down, literally! I challenge the professional to spend quality time in the presence of the Lord in both prayer and fasting and to seek counsel from experienced mentors and spiritual fathers/mothers. I strongly believe that every Christian professional should have a mentor or spiritual father/mother for guidance and great spiritual advice. There is no one that can give you better instruction than a servant of God. We should be reminded that we do not know everything! *"A wise man will hear and increase learning, and a man of understanding will attain wise counsel"* (Proverbs 1:5).

Those in ministry have a tremendous responsibility to make an impact in the life of a juvenile delinquent. The task will not get easier, as the percentage of adolescents conforming to juvenile delinquency will increase while the human birth rate increases. The system will build more juvenile institutions and more children will lose fathers/mothers to crime, death, bogus religions, AIDS, homosexuality, drugs, domestic violence, and many other unpleasant activities. As I write this message to you, my heart is overwhelmed and my eyes are teary because of the great challenge that we have before us.

I write this message as one who holds positions within the church. The world is crying out for help as victims lie trapped in the lion's mouth suffering from pain and fear (especially the juvenile delinquent population). The members of God's church must arise to a new level and increase in God's knowledge, power, and demonstration of the Holy Spirit. We are facing a time when one cannot be stagnant in their ministry because it can cost one their ministry and possibly their life. The servant of God should constantly place themselves in an environment where their tools can be sharpened; they should constantly prepare for warfare. I'm not necessarily advocating for every called individual to attend seminary school. However, I am saying that training is of utmost importance and must be respected by every true servant of the Lord. I encourage the one who is called to walk in their calling with integrity and righteousness. *(Philippians 3:13–14)*

Apostle Paul acknowledged his past, but he did not allow his past to determine who he was in Christ Jesus. If I had allowed every negative thing to defeat me, I would not be where I am today. I would have been defeated. It is true that negative words can be damaging, but they must be observed as obstacles. Any person, place, or thing that is contrary to the mission of God is only a spiritual force that can be destroyed.

I want to share with you a little secret. You may say, "I know," but listen anyway! The key to overcoming these obstacles is prayer. I'm not just talking about any ordinary prayer like religious folks do; I am talking about the kind of prayer that will shake the earth and the dead in the earth and those who walk upon this earth. The type of prayer that can get an answer from God quickly. If you can remember the story of King Hezekiah, you would recall Hezekiah constantly going before the Lord in prayer whenever his enemies came up against him. The bible declares that Hezekiah held fast to the Lord *(II Kings 18:6)*. I believe that because of Hezekiah's obedience and loyalty to the Lord, God honored his petitions that were desperately made to Him. *"The Lord was with him; he prospered wherever he went. And he rebelled against the King of Assyria and did not serve him" (II Kings 18:7).* It was Hezekiah's faithfulness that allowed the Lord to act quickly on his behalf. I believe that when one is totally committed to the Lord with all their heart, mind, and soul, God will supernaturally work in that person's life. God requires us to be faithful, even if it means natural death. *"Christ will be magnified in my body, whether by life or by death" (Philippians 1:20).*

I cannot stress enough the importance of a dynamic prayer life. Prayer is the only method of communication where information is being channeled to God. This means that there is a relationship that is being built. The intimacy comes shortly after a relationship has been identified with Christ. Non-Christians do not comprehend what it means to have an intimate relationship with the Lord, and sometimes, we as Christians struggle with this concept as well. In a biblical sense, the word intimacy pertains to a high level of love that exists between God and His child. To have an intimate relationship with God means that one is highly in love with God and has accepted God's unconditional love, which he offers to humanity.

Abraham had an intimate relationship with God. Abraham's intimacy with God was so potent that he held rapid conversations with the Lord. *"Abraham answered and said, indeed now, I who am but dust and ashes have taken it upon myself to speak to the Lord"* (Genesis 18:27). Abraham realized his imperfections as a man, but he acknowledged that perfection is in the Lord.

I have been active in the ministry for several years, and I have come to the conclusion that God favors those who are humble. The Bible declares that Jesus, *"being found in appearance as a man, He humbled himself and became obedient to the point of death, even the death of the cross"* (Philippians 2:7). Well, guess what? The Lord also wants us to humble ourselves. It's better that we humble ourselves than to be humbled by God. If you want to see God work in your life and ministry, then humble yourself. Humility is a prerequisite in being a servant of God. John the Baptist also knew the importance of humbling himself; he knew if there was going to be any increase, it must come from the Lord.

The problem that many ministries are facing today is that there appears to be a drought in power. Why do you think this drought exists? I believe that it's due to a lack of humility. There have been times in my ministry that I was a little too confident, and as a result, I found myself utilizing human spirit as opposed to Holy Spirit. I find that whenever I submit myself under the authority of the Holy Sprit and welcome God's presence, I see a tremendous explosion of the Holy Spirit.

Servant of GOD, we are in a different dispensation, decade, and generation! We need an increase in power that can only come from obedience to God, prayer, and fasting. The wolves are out hunting to find a servant of God that they can bring to destruction. If they can stop God's servant, they can prevent thousands of souls from being saved just through that particular individual. It is time for the ministries to unfold the authentic power of the Holy Spirit. I am talking about the power to resurrect the dead, heal the sick, and bring deliverance to those who remain in bondage and under the yoke of the adversary.

God must be real to us, and we must obtain a personal relationship with Him. Apostle Paul wrote in the book of *Philippians 3:10, "That I may know him, and the power of his resurrection, and the fellowship of his sufferings, being conformed to His death."* I did not fully understand what this meant until I experienced a divine appointment with the Lord. Historically, I have always been fascinated with sermons and preachers, but I never imagined myself being called into the ministry. It wasn't until I met my wife Keisha that God began to set me up for the ministry. I have heard several prophecies suggest that God was calling me to be a minister, but I never really truly believed that God would call "me" into the ministry. Then, a dynamic experience happened to me in the early morning. On March 3, 1998 at 4:23 A.M., I remember voicing in the bed to the Lord, "Lord when are you going to call me to preach your Word," and suddenly, I saw a great illumination in my bedroom, as if someone had turned on the lights. Keisha was sleeping when I looked over at her. I remembered saying to the Lord, "Your servant is listening," because that is what had been taught to me through Old Testament biblical readings. I was so nervous, I didn't know what to do but pray. After the light left the room, I went out into the living room and began praying on my knees to the Lord. I can't remember the prayer that I said, but I can assure you that I was giving God the Glory!

I went back to bed and at 6:09 A.M., something happened again. My body felt like I was going into a trance. I then heard a voice that said, "Your master is speaking, come into my room." I was in complete shock, but in total obedience to the Lord. I woke Keisha up and asked her if she had seen a light or heard anything, and she said no. I was amazed that God had called me as he had called the Apostle Paul. I tell you one thing, my brothers and sisters, from that day, I have never put down the sword, and I have been on fire for the Lord.

The Lord instructed me to use this as a testimony, and I am. I have told hundreds of people this testimony, and some believe and others are still "religious." A mental health therapist in this field would think that I was experiencing visual and auditory hallucinations. However, it doesn't really offend me when I sense in the spirit that someone does not believe me because I know God for myself, and I have experienced the power of His resurrection! Trust me, if there was not a God, I would not be devoting my entire life in service to Him. There is no one on earth that can convince me that there is no God. I experienced a divine appointment with God of a higher calling. I am absolutely sure of my calling into the ministry, and I am currently active in different segments of the ministry.

Servant of GOD, stop waiting for third confirmations from man to know that you are called into the ministry. God calls man; man cannot call God. If you wait on man to define your ministry, you will be waiting until you experience your last breath upon this earth. God will confirm your ministry and then, it's up to you to prepare yourself and win souls for the Kingdom of God like there is no tomorrow! The clock is ticking, and we do not have a lot of time left to work for the Kingdom of God. Listen to what the book of *Isaiah* states.

> *The Spirit of the Lord God is upon me; because the Lord has anointed me to preach good tidings to the poor; he has sent me to heal the brokenhearted, to proclaim liberty to the captives, and the opening of the prison to those who are bound; to proclaim the acceptable year of the Lord, and the day of vengeance of our God; to comfort all that mourn. (Isaiah 61:1–2)*

To be called into the ministry is the highest calling both in the natural and spiritual realm. There is nothing more important than one's service to God. God must be the center of your life and the life of your family. I often hear people who are called in the ministry indicate that they have a few things in their life to work out prior to them accepting their calling. A message to the wise! Don't let Satan deceive you. The more that you sit on your calling and gifts, the more havoc will occur in your life and in the life of your family. One should not have to experience a traumatic experience in order to accept their calling. Apostle Paul experienced this prior to becoming a Christian. It was not until he actually experienced a Divine encounter with the Lord, where he had no choice but to accept the King of Kings. Saul (Apostle Paul) *"kicked against the pricks"* but eventually became a true soldier for the Kingdom of God and was one of the most devoted apostles.

The adversary will try to discourage you from entering the ministry and with all his craftiness tell you that you will be impoverished. However, do not believe him because God will take care of you and your family. Always remember that Jesus is Jehovah-Jireh (provider), and he will provide for you as he provided for Abraham and all of our brothers and sisters who serve Him.

CHAPTER 10
THE LAST CALL

As a teenager living in Long Island, New York, I can recall having a dream one night that was very powerful and symbolic. In this particular dream, I was running like I'd never imagined I could run. I found myself running after a train that was heading in a particular direction. I became afraid because I desperately wanted to get on the train. The train was traveling at such a fast rate that I became discouraged. After running after this train for a long period of time, I realized that I was not going to make it, but I had a feeling and desire inside to make it on this train. Suddenly, a right hand extended from the front of the train and stretched out in my direction. I grabbed the hand and was pulled up onto the train. At that time, the train proceeded at an even faster rate, and I felt so safe and secure. I remember waking up with a smile on my face, and I felt so peaceful. I began to interpret this dream, and I constantly meditated on this dream day and night.

This dream occurred in my life when I was not saved. Yes, I was attending church, but I was not saved. I did not fully comprehend what salvation meant until I accepted Jesus Christ as my personal Savior and Lord. This is when I fully acknowledged that there was someone who loved me unconditionally. Someone who looked beyond my faults and my imperfection's. Someone who accepted me for who I am and who was willing to use me with the gifts that He had imparted into me.

Well, eventually God gave me an interpretation of the dream. The interpretation is this: The time I spent running meant that I had finally realized that there was something on that train that was worth getting on. In addition, this train was going at an exceedingly fast rate, and I knew that this was the last train. The fast rate of the train symbolized that it had a destination to conquer and was on a time schedule. When I realized that I desired to get on this train, I knew that there was a God and that I wanted to accept Him into my life. When I thought that I would not make it on the train, I realized my limitations and imperfections as man, and I needed and began to internally cry out for help. The hand that stretched out to save me was the Lord Jesus Christ. There was one more thing that God gave me in the interpretation. The reason that I was running so fast was because Satan was chasing me. Satan was mad because I'd decided that I wanted to give my life to the Lord. I was tired of devoting my life to the things of the world where I felt no satisfaction or completeness in happiness. The essence of this dream is simple. It's titled the last call!

There are millions of people who wake up in the morning as if they woke themselves up. People who only want to acknowledge God when something traumatic has happened in their life. It disturbs me how people only want to call on God when they need something tangible. As a minister, the only time I have experienced people in church in abundance is at a wedding or a funeral. Where are the people prior to this? I forgot—you might also see a crowd of people who will come out on Easter Sunday with new suits and dresses on. However, the true purpose of Easter may not be appreciated.

We are living in a time period where people need the Lord, but many are still denying Him. The Bible clearly indicates per Jesus, *"therefore whoever confesses Me before men, him I will also confess also before My father who is in heaven. But whoever denies Me before men, him I will also deny before My father who is in heaven"* (Matthew 10:32–33). Two thousand years later and humans are still denying the existence of Jesus Christ, the true and only Messiah. I often wonder, how long will this continue? Here is a message to the unsaved: Jesus is coming again, and He is returning as a judge. I can tell you one thing, as I have told several unsaved people in the world. If one had a little intelligence, they would accept Jesus just to be on the safe side! You do not have to be a college graduate to know if there is a God! Of course Jesus knows our heart, and He acknowledges who is authentic and who is not when it concerns salvation. There is a great void in the life of the unbeliever, and if not filled righteously, they will fill it with fruits of unrighteousness. It is true that it is important for Christians to display patience with the unsaved when regarding the duration of acceptance of Jesus. It's easy for one to be passionate about a soul that has gone astray. I believe that any person who does not believe that there is a God is blind. Allow me to go a step further. Any person who does not believe that Jesus has been resurrected from the dead is surely spiritually unhealthy and is in need of Christian life. *(Romans 10:9–10)*

God lays out a formula for the children that he created. It's an easy formula to understand and apply. The ingredients are very plain, simple, and self-explanatory to the one who has the Spirit of meekness. There can be no fabricated formula to replace the original. I'm trying to say that Jesus is the only way. The Bible declares that *"Jesus said to him, I am the way, the truth, and the life. No one comes to the Father except through Me"* (John 14:6). I have learned that the foods that taste tremendously good in the restaurants are sometimes challenging to get recipes for, but becoming a Christian has a recipe that has been both printed and preached on a consistent basis. This recipe is available for all those who have an appetite for a taste that is GOOD! *"O taste and see that the Lord is good; blessed is the man who trusts in Him"* (Psalm 34:8).

As a young man called into the ministry, I have learned something special about the concept of "time." I have learned that time does not wait for anyone or anybody! Time is an existence that must happen and is unavoidable. One cannot stop the process of time or even speed up the process of time. Time is what it is. Time cannot be negotiated or traded for goods or other insignificant items that earth offers. Time cannot be purchased with the most beautiful and expensive diamond in the world. Time cannot be debated with the most elite and notorious philosophers in this world. Time must be respected and appreciated. Time allows one the instant motivation to act, whether in a positive or negative manner. If we apply the concept of time with our current societal juvenile delinquent status, one can see that delinquents have not fully comprehended the loyalty of time. This does not just pertain to juveniles but also adults. Most importantly, juveniles are violating time for many reasons.

As a child, I was such a devoted basketball player. I spent quality time playing basketball on a daily and nightly basis. I was so devoted to playing basketball that I can recall several occasions of playing basketball outdoors in the snow, ice, and rain. There was no stopping me whenever I had a basketball in my hand. I became one of the top high school basketball players in the country, and I attended invitational basketball summer camps. I believe that I accomplished this success because I was willing to utilize my time wisely. I devoted my time daily to playing, reading, and thinking and eating basketball. I am not discussing these things to boast in the flesh, but I'm boasting in the Lord! At that time in my life, it was basketball that was going to determine my future. The sport became so important to me that I was willing to dedicate my time to this game. Well, this is how one should demonstrate their love to Jesus. One should be able to turn their life completely over to Him. In addition, one should devote one's entire life in establishing an authentic relationship with Him and converting to His will! There is no age requirement. It does not matter if you are five, eighteen, eighty, or a hundred years of age. God will accept you as you are! Time is running out and it's time for people to be decisive about God, just like one is decisive about other variables in one's life. When Elijah instructed Ahab to send the 450 prophets of Baal to Mount Carmel, Elijah challenged the decision making process of the false prophets. *(I Kings 18:21)*

According to the text, the scripture mentions that the false prophets answer Elijah not a word. It would be appropriate to state that they made a decision in their minds and heart not to follow the Lord. Unfortunately, there were major consequences that resulted in following the god of Baal. It cost the prophets their lives and their souls because they served the god that was inferior to the King of Kings and the Lord of Lords. The Bible explains that the prophets of Baal began to cut themselves with knives and lancets until blood gushed out of their bodies. Now you explain this to me, because I may need a little help in digesting this. What loving God would allow you to cause pain to yourself? Not Jesus! Jesus will not allow you to afflict bodily harm to yourself or others.

The problem that many unsaved people are faced with today is that their pain is unhealed because of their lack of salvation in Christ. This is not the time to experiment with the gods of this world. The liberty that God has given us is being abused and used in an improper manner. Humanity has a way of "pushing things to the limit." Well, that's exactly what people are doing today. To be more specific, that's exactly what juvenile delinquents are doing with the Lord. They are putting God off to see what they can get away with. This means if they can get away with murder, than it's just possible that they may make a decision to murder someone in the heat of opportunity.

God's grace is sufficient! I have always been amazed by how much patience God displays with humanity. Have you thought about the role a doctor plays in your life? A person will usually go to a doctor when something is wrong with their physical body or when they want to have an annual examination. You rarely hear about a doctor initially making a call to a client's residence to see if they and their family are feeling fine. This type of doctor-to-patient relationship does not really exist today. There are even times when a patient goes to the doctor and sees everybody else but the doctor! HERE'S THE UNIQUE THING ABOUT THE DOCTOR! The doctor knows that eventually you will decide to come in for a visitation. He knows that you are only human and that the body is susceptible to various medical issues. You may try all kinds of home remedies to cure your sickness, but eventually, you will just have to make a visit to the doctor for professional help.

Well, if you will view this scenario from a Christian perspective, God is the supernatural physician. He allows you the freedom to experience just about everything one's heart wants to experience. He waits and waits patiently for you to make a change for righteousness. Then circumstances begin to occur in your life. These circumstances may entail a death of a loved one, dissatisfaction of the world, sickness, lack of life's necessities, internal pain, unhappiness, relationship and marital problems, drug and alcohol addiction, etc. The list can go on and on, but I'm sure you get the point! Jesus will wait to the point where you have picked every habit and style that the world influences, until you decide to pick up the cross! For some it may take years and for others it may be a quick decision. God's unconditional love is forever present as he continues to wait patiently. He can provide all that life fails to offer and sustain.

For the most part, I find that there are more individuals who are afraid of God than those individuals who actually fear Him.

There is a difference. The person who is afraid of God is usually the one who is functioning outside the will of God. This person has decided that they are going "to live their own life" and do whatever they desire to do when they want to do it! This individual is usually not concerned about consequences, although they may have sensitivity about the wrath of God and are willing to take as many chances as possible. On the contrary, you have the person who is God-fearing. This particular individual is the one who obeys the voice of God in His commandments and biblical principles. This person desires to consistently be in the presence of God and seeks higher spiritual growth and relations. This individual is reluctant to disappoint the Lord because of the spiritual fulfillment he/she acquires when they are inclined to the Holy Spirit. This person has decided to accept their designed and ultimately ordained calling from God.

Time is running short and you cannot win the race unless you are in the race. Are we all ready for the Kingdom of God? This is one question that can only be answered by two parties. Jesus and the individual are the only ones who can provide answers to this question. According to the New Testament book of *Revelation*, John was on the isle of Patmos, while in the Spirit he received revelation from the Lord regarding the end time. The rapture is a party for Christians, but not for the unbeliever. Chapter four of the book of *Revelation* discusses the actual rapture that will occur at God's appointed time.

> *After these things I looked, and behold, a door standing open in heaven. And the first voice which I heard was like a trumpet speaking with me, saying come up here, and I will show you things which must take place after this. (Revelation 4:1)*

This is a wonderful time for the Christian population—a time of celebration for being faithful to the God of the Heavens and the God of creation. Throughout sections of the book of *Revelation*, John mentions how he also saw a new heaven and earth while he was in the Spirit. *(Revelation 21:1–2)*

The benefits of a Christian life are eternally unlimited. As Christian professionals, we are obligated to impart these benefits to the unsaved and those who have not answered to the call. We should remind them that God is a God who has a mission to save their soul from eternal damnation. It is not too late, but the time is running!

Prior to doing an altar call after preaching a sermon, I usually ask the individuals to close their eyes while the Lord uses me to extend an invitation to salvation. Some eyes are closed, some peek, and others just do not comply with instructions. I also talk about the day when every knee shall bow before the Lord and acknowledge that HE IS LORD! There are some that positively respond to this and there are others who fail to receive the invitation for salvation and eternal life with the Lord. There are times when the Lord would tell me that there are more within the congregation who are unsaved, and I will proceed in doing another altar call. Some would accept, but still the others would remain in their seat unsure. I often wonder what causes these individuals to remain in their chairs after the Word of God went forth and an altar call was made for them to inherit eternal life in the Kingdom of God. I must be honest with you because at times it could really be puzzling to me! I have evidence to believe that people who hear the Word of God are reluctant to be saved for a few reasons that will be listed in this book.

This is a very exciting time for Christians who have committed their lives to serving God. It's wonderful knowing that you will one day walk on streets of gold, enjoy your loved ones, and eat fruit from the tree of life, among many other beautiful experiences in the presence of God. God wants the unbeliever to be a part of this. He continues to knock on the door for entrance into one's heart. He wants to give you a peace that will pass all your understanding and impart unlimited blessings in your life. His desire is for you to be with Him. *(Revelation 3:20–22)*

Saturday June 29, 2002 at 1:30 P.M. was the day of my grandmother's (Louise L. Ellison) home going service (funeral). The home going service was taking place at a church in Jamaica. It was a nice church located in the country of St. Toolies—a place in the country that not many people have heard of. It was challenging for me because I was one of the officiating ministers and the one who preached the sermon at the service. I never felt such a great anointing in a church as I did that afternoon. The small sized church was packed as sardines in a can. The exciting thing about the service was that family, relatives, friends, and almost the entire community attended the service. The church choir was on fire, the pastor was fired up, and the church audience was clapping and jumping to the rhythm of the songs and music. It was evident that God was surely in that place. The reason why everyone was so happy was that we knew in our hearts that Grandmother was home with the Lord. We had every reason to celebrate. At the end of the message, we did an altar call, and I asked those who desired to receive Jesus Christ as their personal Savior to raise their hand. In front of my eyes, I witnessed my own family and friends of the family raise their hands and accept Jesus Christ that afternoon. It was so wonderful to know that my grandmother was in the presence of the Lord and to see family accept the Lord in their life.

There are some people who could not comprehend why one would do an altar call at a funeral service. To the religious one, this action can be perceived as strange. However, to the Christian, this is normal procedure. There are many people who just do not understand their purpose in life. As said a little earlier, many believe that they are on earth to gain a career, get rich, party, as well as other activities that this world offers. This is a big deception from Satan. Satan wants to continue to delay the unbeliever. If you are an unbeliever and you are reading this book, I want you to know that Satan has a contract on your soul for eternal damnation. He wants you to be tormented for eternity and will continue to paint that wonderful picture of the world's fleshly offerings. If you fall into this category, I also want you to know that this contract can be broken. The only way it can be broken is by accepting Jesus into your life and by allowing the blood of Jesus to cover you—the blood that Jesus shed on the cross. It is no concern what one's secular status is or how rich or famous you may be. The only way you can make it into the Kingdom is by acknowledging Jesus Christ as your Lord. *(Revelation 1:7–8)*

Jesus is surely returning! Are you ready? This question is for every human that walks the face of this earth, including myself. As Christians, I believe that one of the beautiful things about not knowing when Jesus will return is that we have to repent daily of our sins. If you think about it, all of us have been convicted in our lives for doing something that was not the right thing. This could have been lying on your income tax or not attending church intentionally for several months. As Christians, we should stay in constant relationship with God. This will enable one to want to improve in the areas of their life that are deficient. Holiness is a process and does not occur overnight; it cannot be purchased over the counter of a pharmacy. One can work towards Holiness by studying the Word and applying the Word to one's life. If you fall down within the process, then get back up and continue running the race!

If you are an unbeliever, I want you to know that Jesus loves you. You may have many flaws and imperfections, but He still loves you. You may have used drugs, been involved with crime, practiced homosexuality, or worshipped false gods. God loves you more than a human can imagine. I challenge you to draw close to God who is the resurrection. In the New Testament, Jesus said to Martha, *"I am the resurrection. He who believes in Me, though he may die, he shall live: And whoever lives and believes in Me shall never die" (John 11:25–26)*. The following two pages contain a list of reasons why people are reluctant to accept Jesus Christ as their Savior and Lord, as well as why people turn their lives over to Jesus.

WHY PEOPLE ARE RELUCTANT TO ACCEPT JESUS AS THEIR LORD AND SAVIOR

- Lack of basic biblical knowledge
- Feelings of guilt
- Anger towards God for a particular reason(s)
- Unable to flee from youthful lust and pleasures of the world
- Think that they have to get their life in order first
- Previous negative church experiences and encounters with Christians
- Misconceptions about Christianity
- Concern about what others would think about them
- Feel they don't need God in their life
- Difficulties denying themselves selfish goals and desires

WHY PEOPLE ARE WILLING TO ACCEPT JESUS AS THEIR LORD AND SAVIOR

- Come to realize that Jesus offers unconditional love
- To inherit eternal life with the Father, Son, and Holy Spirit
- Jesus died for their sins of the world
- They received the gospel in meekness
- Have been trained in the Word of God from early developmental stages
- Tired of the offerings of the world
- Have exhausted all earthly resources and hit rock bottom
- Believe in their heart that Jesus was raised from the dead and that He is Lord
- Need an authentic and true friend in their life
- Experienced a Divine Intervention from the Lord

The above lists, consisting of the reasons why people choose to accept or not accept Jesus as their Lord and Savior, are only a few reasons. I wanted you to see some of the reasons that apply to each category.

As a minister of the gospel, I have heard several different excuses for why people reject Jesus. I find that unbelievers do themselves a great injustice by rejecting their creator. Life brings great challenges, circumstances, crisis, and diverse disasters. A human is only made up of 206 bones in the human anatomy. If you think about it, what are 206 bones compared to the God of the universe, who cannot be measured by width, height, or depth? Where can humanity mobilize without God? Where can he hide and where can she run? The juvenile delinquent should become aware of the great limitations and weakness of mankind and be encouraged to accept the avenue of becoming a *"Real Servant"* for the Lord! Juveniles should be able to open their eyes and see the darkness and gloomy paths of their choice(s). The light of this world must overcome this gloominess and impart sunshine to the eclipsed vessel of humanity.

I have learned that the package of gifts that God has granted us should not be utilized for the things of no prominence, but they should be used for the development of dysfunctional beings. Let the Spirit of God take you to higher heights and deeper depths than life automatically offers. Juvenile delinquents not only need community services but they need to be serviced with the heavenly love of Jesus Christ.

I pray that this book was a blessing to you and that it will challenge the mind and heart of the believer and inherit the unbeliever to the Kingdom of God. I also encourage the Christian professional to stay keen to the many changes in their community that affect the realm of juvenile delinquency. Its important to remember that God loves you unconditionally and wants to perfect you as a soldier armed for eternity affairs! I will leave you with a scripture verse that has spiritually motivated me to work laboriously for the Kingdom of God in the appointed time I have been allotted on earth. *"Lord make me to know mine end, and the measure of my days, what it is; that I may know how frail I am"* (*Psalm 39:4*).

RECOMMENDATIONS

Individuals who work with juvenile delinquents have a great level of responsibility. The intensity of juvenile delinquents will increase if a Divine Intervention is not presented to them. Christians should be willing to shine their lights in the midst of a dark world, a world that is comfortable in its mental, physical, and spiritual condition. Juvenile delinquents must be encouraged and informed about a lively hope, which is Christ Jesus! Spiritual leaders should be equipped with essential skills and techniques sufficiently sharp to alleviate the weight that burdens the delinquent adolescent. The future presents a harvest of souls crying out to be saved from a pit of excruciating internal pain. As laborers for the Lord, let our last words include, *"I have fought a good fight, I have finished my course, I have kept the faith: now there is laid up for me a crown of righteousness" (2 Timothy 4:7–8).*

BIBLIOGRAPHY

Anastasi, G. (1990). God's Answer to Depression. New York: Word of Life Ministries.

Bailey, W. C. (1996). Less-than-lethal weapons and police—citizen killings in U.S. urban areas. Crime & Delinquency, 42(4), 535-552.

Bartol, C.R. (1989). Juvenile Delinquency A Systems Approach. New Jersey: Prentice-Hall, Inc.

Begun, A.M. (1999). Growing up in America. Texas: Information Plus.

Bender, D.L. (1999). Teen At Risk. California: Green Haven Press.

Bishop, D.M. (1996). The transfer of juveniles to criminal court: does it make a difference? Crime & Delinquency, 42(2), 171-191.

Bole, W. (1994). Today's minister: the key to ministering to youths: the models and lots of guidance and support from parents. Nations Catholic Reporter, 30(12), 1-2.

Bright, W. (1996). Black father's perspectives. Urban Education, 31(3), 247-260.

Brock, P. (1992). The "no-future" generation? The Ecumenical Review, 44(2), 1-2.

Casey, R. D. & Caor, L. (1983). Group work with hard-to-reach adolescents: the use of member initiated program selection. Social Work With Groups, 6(1), 9-22.

Cicourel, A. V. (1995). The Social Organization of Juvenile Justice. New Jersey: Transaction Publishers.

Corey, G. (1990). <u>Theory and Practice of Group Counseling</u>. California: Brooks Publishing.

Damphousse, K.R. & Crouch, B. (1992). Did the devil make them do it? <u>Youth & Society, 24</u>(2), 204-224.

Demo, R. (1993). Crack cocaine dealing by adolescents in two public housing projects. <u>Human Organization, 52</u>(1), 89–96.

Edwards, C. (1999). Wicca casts spells on teen-age girls. <u>Insight on the News, 15,</u> (139), 22-26.

Elkind, D. & Walli, B. The ongoing journey awakening spiritual life in at-risk youth. Nebraska: Boystown Press.

Ellis, A. (1985). Overcoming resistance. Rational-emotive therapy with difficult clients. New York: Springs Publishing.

Field, B. C. (1999). Bad kids. New York: Oxford University Press, Inc.

Fleener, F. T. (1999). Family and factor in delinquency. <u>Psychological Reports, 85</u>, 80–81.

Frame, R. L. (1994). Networking for peace. <u>Christianity Today, 38</u>(9), 23.

Fremon, C. (1995). Father Greg and the homeboys. New York: USA.

Hawes, J. M. (1971). Children in urban society. New York: Oxford University Press.

Heath, S. B. & McLaughlin, M. W. (1993). Identity and inner-city youth. New York: Teachers College Press.

Hill, D. (1997). Eyewitness books witches and magic-makers. New York: Alfred A. Knopt. Inc.

Jackson, C. (1996). Straight talk on tough topics. Michigan: Zondervan Publishing House.

Jacob, H. (1980). Crime and justice in urban America. New Jersey: Prentice Hall, Inc.

James, K. (1798). The Holy Bible. Nashville: Thomas Nelson.

Jeffrey, C. R. (1998). Prevention of juvenile violence: a critical review of current scientific strategies. Journal of Offender Rehabilitation, 28(1/2), 1-28.

Jenkins, R. L. & Brown, W. K. (1988). The abandonment of delinquent behavior. Promoting the turn around. New York: Praeger Publishers.

Johnson, K. (1998). Preventing and reducing alcohol and other drug use among high-risk youths by increasing family resilience. Social Work, 43(4), 297.

Johnson, W. B. (1993). Christian rational-emotive therapy: a treatment protocol. Journal of Psychology and Christianity, 12(3), 254-261.

Jones, D. P. H. (1997). What do children know about religion and Satanism? Child Abuse and Neglect, 21(11), 109.

Kalljee, L. M. (1995). Urban African American adolescents and their parents: perceptions of violence within and against their communities. Human Organization, 54(4), 373.

Kaplan, H. L., Sadick, B. T., & Grebb, J. A. (1994). Synopsis of Psychiatry. Maryland: Williams & Wilkins.

Khanna, J. L. (1975). New Testament approaches to juvenile delinquency. Illinois: Thomas Publisher.

Kipke, M. D. (1997). Street youth, their peer group affiliation and differences according to residential status, subsistence patterns, and use of services. Adolescence, 32(127), 655-670.

Koteskyey, R. L., Little, M. D. & Matthews, M. V. (1991). Adolescent identity and depression. Journal of Psychology and Christianity, 10(1), 48–53.

Kvaraceus, W. C. & Ulrich, W. E. (1960). Delinquent's behavior. Washington, D.C.: U.S.

Larsen, E. (1989). Overcoming depressive living syndrome. Missouri: Triumph Books.

Leechan, J. (1989). Pastoral care for survivors of family abuse. Kentucky: Westminister / John Knox Press.

Levinson, R. B. & Greene III, J.J. (1999). New "boys" on the block: a study of prison inmates under the age of 18. Corrections Today, 61(1), 60 – 64.

Lipsker, L. E., & Dordi, R. M. (1990). Treatment of depression in adolescents: a Christian cognitive-behavior therapy approach. Journal of Psychology and Christianity, 9(4), 25-33.

Liston, A. A. (1997). Tennis shoes tax stamina for justice. National Catholic Reporter, 34(2), 1-2.

Lowney, K. S. (1995). Teenage Satanism as oppositional youth subculture. Journal of Contemporary Ethnography, 23(4), 453–468.

McRoberts, O.M. (1999). Understanding the "new" black pentecostal activism: lessons from ecumenical urban ministries. Sociology of Religion, 60(1), 47 – 50.

Meltzer, M. (1999). Witches and witch hunts. New York: The Blue Sky Press.

Miller, S. J. (1994). Juvenile justice in America. New Jersey: Regents / Prentice Hall, Inc.

Myers, L. G. (1994). Common goals are key to juvenile justice system success. Corrections Today, 56(7), 100–104.

Narramore, C. M. (1960). The psychology of counseling. U.S.: Zondervan Publishing.

Nesessary, J. R. & Parishi, T. S. (1995). Relationships of parents': perceived actions toward their children. Adolescence, 30(117), 1–3.

Osborne, R. (1998). Talking to your children about God. New York: Harper-Collins Publishers.

Ottens, A. J. & Myer, R. A. (1994). Coping with Satanism. Rosen Publishing Group, Inc.

Packer, J. I. (2000). Is Satan Omnipresent? Christianity Today, 44(10), 115.

Parks, W. (200).[Query: 2000] Victory over hexes, spells, and curses. USA

Patterson, C. H. (1986). Theories of counseling and psychotherapy. New York: Harper Collins Publishers.

Paulson, S. E. & Sputa, C. L. (1996). Patterns of parenting during adolescence: perceptions of adolescents and parents. Adolescence, 31(122), 370 – 380.

Rojek, D. G. (1996). Exploring delinquency causes and control. California: Roxbury Publishing Company.

Rubin, R. H., Billingsley, A. & Caldwell, C. H. (1994). The role of the black church in working with black adolescents. Adolescence, 29(114), 251-267.

Savicki, V. & Brown, R. (1981). Working with troubled children. New York: Human Sciences Press.

Schellenbach, C. J. & Trickett, P. K. (1998). Violence against children in the family and the community. American Psychological Association. Washington, D. C.: Limber & Nation.

Schultz, D. & Schultz, E. S. (1994). Theories of personality. California: Brooks Publishing.

Seamands, D. A. (1991). Healing for damaged emotions. U.S.: SP Publications.

Shaw, C. R. (1972). Juvenile delinquency and urban areas. Chicago: University of Chicago.

Spiegler, M. (1996). Marketing street culture: bringing hip-hop style to the mainstream. American Demographics, 18(11). 28 – 35.

Steinberg, L. & Levine, A. (1990). You and your adolescent. A parents guide for ages 10 to 20. New York: Harper Collins Publishers, Inc.

Sullivan, L.Y. (1997). Hip-hop nation: the undeveloped social capital of black urban America. National Civic Review, 86(3), 253 – 262.

Tapia, A. (1995). The power of the painted word: how an urban youth transformed city wall to communicate life and hope. Christianity Today, 39(8), 67 – 69.

Taylor, S. (1997). Adolescent's perceptions of family

responsibility-taking. Adolescence, 32(128), 970 – 976.

Vuchinjch, S. (1996). Family experience in pre-adolescence and in developments of male delinquency. Journal of Marriage and the Family, 58, 491 – 501.

Wallis, J. (1997). With unconditional love. Sojourners, 26(5). 16 – 23.

Wernick, R. (1999). Who the devil is the devil? Smithsonian, 30(7), 112-120.

Wilkinson, A. R. (1994). State, local initiatives target at risk youths. Corrections Today, 56(7), 92 – 95.

Yalom, I. D. (1975). The theory and practice of group psychotherapy. New York: Basic Books.

Young, P. V. & Pound, R. (1969). Social treatment in probation and delinquency. New Jersey: Patterson Smith.

ABOUT THE AUTHOR

Paul Campbell has been used in many capacities within the ministry. He has a bachelor's degree in Criminal Justice from Gannon University in Erie, Pennsylvania, Masters degree in Rehabilitation Counseling from the University of South Florida, as well as a Doctorate in Ministry from Logos Christian College and Graduate School in Jacksonville, FL. He has served as a pastor, teacher, evangelist, and church planter. His devotion and commitment towards winning souls and sharpening ministers of the gospel have played a significant part in his ministerial contributions. He has a tremendous heart in seeing people surrender to Jesus Christ and live a holistic Christian life that includes a spiritual relationship with God, adequate family life, pursuit of academics, and exploring recreational activities. He is a License Mental Health Counselor who works part-time in private practice. Paul is devoted in working with individuals with existing counseling issues and is currently a ministerial team player at Celebration Church in Jacksonville, Florida. His greatest excitement is spending quality time with his beautiful wife Keisha and his lovely daughters Genesis, Naomi and Hannah who all give him great joy, inspiration and motivation.

Paul Campbell can be contacted for services at:
pcampbell@counselingsolutioninc.com